MW01615359

When Life Knocks the Hell Out of You
Beat the Odds

The Story. The People. The Pain. The Love.
The Final Triumph
Over a Paralyzing Football Injury.

A sports story for moms, dads,
coaches and kids. It's my story.

Joe Rhea

First Edition: March 2021
When Life Knocks the Hell Out of You:
Beat the Odds

Foreword by
Adam Teicher, ESPN National Sports Writer

Events described in these stories are drawn from actual experience.

Cover Design: Randy Lackey
Interior Design: Randy Lackey/Covington Group

Joe Rhea@JoeRhea.com

For my daughter Molly Jayne
The light of my life.

BY ADAM TEICHER,
ESPN NATIONAL SPORTS REPORTER

It's never easy when the dreams of a professional sports career die, no matter how it happens.

It's tough enough when it happens naturally, when it's proven someone just doesn't have the proper ability or simply doesn't want to put in the work that it takes to get there. But when those dreams are taken away by a debilitating injury? That's the most difficult situation of all.

That's what happened to my good friend Joe Rhea, whose dreams were ended at age 14 when a collision on the football field changed everything. Maybe Joe wouldn't have become a professional athlete without the injury. Maybe he would have made it. I would have bet on Joe to become a major league baseball player.

Either way, that's not the point. Joe was unable to take it to the proper finish, one way or the other, to find out. The important thing, as you will see in his inspirational story, is that the injury wasn't the end for Joe. He takes you through his difficult rehab, one filled with plenty of physical and emotional pain, and shifted his focus and his energy to areas other than sports.

And Joe's journey wasn't without its light-hearted moments. One happens shortly after his accident, when a fellow hospital patient asks Joe, still wearing his halo from the accident, "Why you got screws in your head?"

I didn't know whether to laugh or cry. Joe's story will have you doing plenty of both and in the end, you'll feel like you know him, which I'm proud to say I do.

MY THANKS

Without the help and encouragement of friends and mentors, this book would still be in a notebook as it had been for years. I thank everyone who has helped and influenced me along the way. First is my mother, Judi. I thank you, Mom, and always remember the patience, love and support you have given me, not just as a kid, but for my entire life.

High on my list of gratitude is ESPN Sports Reporter Adam Teicher. We met in a coffee shop years ago and spent many days drinking coffee and talking sports. Those were some of my best mornings! I value your friendship Adam, and I'm proud of the foreword you willingly wrote for this book. I'm also grateful for local writer Martha McCarty. You believed in me at a time when I needed it. You cheered me on and renewed my intention to finish writing my story and find a path to a publisher. Without that, this book would not have come to fruition.

Thank you, Andre, my best friend! You're not written into these chapters, but you know you've been a friend in my life since seventh grade. You were Best Man in my marriage to my daughter Molly's mother and you are like my brother—a brother from another mother.

I'm thankful for those who became characters in these stories, including my dad and baseball great Frank White, college friends, the girls I've loved, the neurosurgeon who treated the injury that changed life forever and Bob, the physical therapist who was at my side when I first stood on my legs and struggled to walk again. Even though not all my friends and mentors are named personally, you've all stuck with me through thick and thin.

I don't know where I would be without everyone of you.

Patient became nauseous after the
insertion of the screws within the skull.
Boy has tremendous drive and spirit.
Just what he will need.

(Neurosurgery Specialist's Report for Joe Rhea, age 14.)

A NOTE TO MY READERS

I wish I could tell you that when I sat down to write this book many many years ago, I wanted to write it for all the right reasons. That would be a lie. I wanted to tell the story of an accomplished athlete who overcame herculean feats after a paralyzing football injury when I was fourteen, but as I aged and as the book sat with no new edits or additions, I realized being self-indulgent was not the story I wanted to convey.

There will always be part of me that feels I wanted to be known for my physical, athletic accomplishments. Today, I prefer to share my story with the goal of helping you, the reader, realize that you can suffer more than you thought possible, endure tremendous hardships and disappointments and all the while still be a decent and kind human being. The truth is, there is not a single person on this planet that I know of who has not or will not at some point experience physical or mental pain and trauma. An old proverb credited to the Dalai Lama says, "Pain is inevitable. Suffering is optional."

I can't remember a time when I was a young boy that I didn't want to be a professional athlete. Professional athletes were and still are treated like royalty. That seemed like a good path to follow, but my injury shattered my dreams and left questions that haunted me for years. Did I have the talent? Was being a professional athlete really the path for me? I will never have an answer.

Finally, after writing and rewriting, I have published my first book, a memoir. There is an emotional component in writing honestly and it is difficult opening myself up to the world. I share moments with you that I am not proud of and, at times, ashamed of. Then a critic who read advance chapters sent an awesome comment to me: "Wow! This book is heart-wrenching, thought-provoking and beautiful."

That one single accolade encouraged me. It made me feel that, yes, this is the book I needed to write.

JoeRhea@JoeRhea.com

CHAPTER ONE

LIKE FRANK

I remember it like it was yesterday. It was a late afternoon on a crisp fall October day in 1978. I was sitting on the couch watching TV when a man knocked on the door of my old, ugly brown and green duplex on 809 Medford Circle in Olathe, Kansas. I answered it. I opened the door somewhat cautiously and my eyes climbed upwards and there in front of me stood the second baseman for the Kansas City Royals, Frank White, my favorite baseball player in the entire world! Frank was smiling in his perfectly-pressed gray wool suit as he looked down at me. Who would have thought in a million years that my favorite All-Star professional baseball player would be standing at my door, a kid who dreamed I could one day be like Frank.

For an 8-year-old, the smallest kid on the block, I held onto my dream, but I worried. I thought, *I'll never be big enough to play in the big leagues.*

How did Frank White end up at my front door? He met my mother. That's how.

In his free time off the field one day, Frank went in to renew the lease on his car at John Chezik Buick, a prominent Kansas City dealership. John Chezik was a local icon who partnered with the Royals to offer deals to players who bought or leased a vehicle. When Frank walked in and sat down to renew his lease, the Leasing Manager at the desk was my mother, Judi, and she recognized the man sitting across from her was, in fact, her son's favorite player.

After she went over lease documents with Frank, Mom told me she had mentioned to Frank how much I idolized him and that my love for him and baseball started with the many hot summer nights when

I sat in the backyard with my grandpa listening to Royals baseball games on the local radio station KCSP 610am Sports. That was one of my favorite summer pastimes with Grandpa Pat. When the Royals were not on television, Grandpa and I sat outside and he smoked his cigarettes and drank his beer. Grandpa was a World War II Navy vet, so when he told me Frank White was his favorite player, it was much later in life that I saw how ironic that was since Grandpa was a bit of a racist, maybe a product of his generation. I remember most that he told me Frank White was what he called a "throwback player." I had no idea what he meant.

"What's a throwback player, Grandpa?"

"A throwback player, Joey (they called me Joey), is a ball player that reminds me of the players that played years ago…players that hustle, run hard to first base no matter what when a ball is hit…a player that isn't afraid to slide into second base and break up a double play. A ball player that does the little things, Joey. Bunts, hits the cut-off man, does everything he can to always help the team win."

I knew I was smaller than all the other boys, but I wanted to believe I could always be that kind of player.

Back in the leasing office, Frank listened to Mom tell him of my adoration for him. That's when she took a chance and said, "I know it might not be as exciting as your usual public appearances, but it would mean the world to Joey if you could possibly come and meet him."

"It would be my honor to do that for your son."

Years later, I had the opportunity to ask Frank why he had said yes, he'd come to my house. He said, he thought, *What if Willie Mays, my favorite player, had shown up at my door? It might be the greatest surprise a boy could have ever dreamt of.*"

As he had promised, Frank stood at my door in the dim light of that one autumn evening. I was overwhelmed with excitement. It never even occurred to me that my home was not a showpiece, or that it might look different from what a famous athlete lived in. I was unaware of adult concerns, like financial statements, past-due notices, half-filled gas tanks or chipped paint on the sides of our duplex. I beamed with pride to have Frank White come to our house. I had never felt so special or alive in all eight years of my life.

It seemed that Frank was at complete ease and unhurried. My mother and I invited him in and Frank and I sat down side-by-side on our faded orange and brown sofa, a very 1970s style, if I recall. Since Mom had known this was planned, she had already ordered Godfather's pizza for our dinner. When Frank grabbed a slice of pizza, my first thought was how extremely large his hands were. In typical 8-year-old boy fashion, I said, "You have huge hands!"

"Joey, that's not polite," Mom said. Frank laughed. "It's okay, really," he said. He held up one hand and I put my hand up to his to see how they compared. Mine wasn't even as large as his palm. I handed him my baseball to hold and his hand covered the entire ball. Then I blurted out, "I hate the Yankees! Those damn Yankees!"

He chuckled. I grinned.

The Yankees had defeated the Royals in 1976, '77 and '78. Each playoff series was exciting, each team equally matched and every year, I thought the Royals would win the World Series.

"Mr. White, can I ask you a question?"

"Sure you can."

"Why do the Royals keep losing to the Yankees? We're better than they are! What went wrong this time?"

"Joe, you can call me Frank," he said. "I wish I could give you the right answer. We played our hardest, did our best, but the Yankees were able to make a few more plays than we did. So they beat us again. Even when you play your hardest, do your very best, sometimes you still lose.

"Joe, we have no regrets. Do you know why we have no regrets losing to the Yankees again, Joe?

"Because we know that we did our very best, played the hardest we could, left nothing on the table. While we are all very sad that we lost, we are also very proud, because we can walk away knowing we did everything we could to win. Does that make sense?"

"I think so." (His words rang true two years later when the Royals won in the playoffs against the Yankees, and five years later when they won the World Series against the St. Louis Cardinals.)

Sitting around on the couch that day, Frank and I woofed down the pepperoni pizza piled with cheese while Mom sat quietly, as if she had never seen me happier.

"How did you make it to the big leagues?"

"I was born in Mississippi, but we moved to Kansas City when I was in second grade. I started playing baseball while I grew up here. My grandpa and grandma were sharecroppers and lived on a farm and I was sent back to Mississippi in the summer to help my grandparents and to keep me out of trouble. I picked cotton and did a number of other things."

I thought, *Picking cotton is what made Frank's hands really strong.* Then out of nowhere, I asked more questions like only an 8-year-old would. "Were you afraid of Goose Gossage? He throws the ball 100 miles per hour!" I knew the stats. Gossage was a famed All-Star, a powerful hard-throwing relief pitcher for the Yankees.

"Would you be sacred?" Frank asked me.

"Oh yeah."

"I'm a little nervous when I walk up to the plate. But I have to rely on my training and trust that it will pay off," Frank said. "Hitting a baseball is hard, Joe. It's about timing the pitch just right so the bat meets the ball at the right time, Joe."

I liked it when Frank called me Joe. And I could call him Frank. It made me feel special and grown up. Like an equal, if only for little while.

"It doesn't matter how fast the ball is pitched as long as you time it correctly. I don't ever walk up to bat worried about being hit by a pitch," he told me. "Yes, it happens, but it's rare and those are the best pitchers in the world. They know what they're doing."

He gave me a wink as though he had just shared a very important secret with me. That's how I took it anyway.

In those days, one of the best players in all of baseball was George Brett. He was the third baseman for the Royals and Frank's teammate. Brett was later inducted into the Baseball Hall of Fame and is considered one of the greatest players of all time. Some of you remember the infamous Pine Tar game in 1983 when Brett hit a home run and gave the Royals a one-run advantage over the Yankees. Goose was the pitcher that Brett hit the homer off of, only to have it taken away because umpires ruled there was too much pine tar on Brett's bat. But Frank was still my favorite player and he was sitting in my living room. Yet, I just had to know.

"What do you think about George Brett?"

"He's a great player, and an even better teammate. But what I would want you to know about George is how he does all the little things great. He's what you call a real throwback player."

"That's what my grandpa says about you!"

"Well, your grandpa sounds like he knows what he's talking about. Watch Brett's routine at the plate while he prepares for each pitch. Watch how he hustles to first base even when it's just a routine ground ball that he hit. No matter, he runs as hard as he can. You know why he does that?

"It's because you never know what will happen. The infielder might make an error, the ball may take a bad bounce. If it's a pop up, the wind can blow the ball away. The point is, Joe, if you aren't running as hard as you can, they might still be able to throw you out at first. George always runs hard, as I do. His head is always in the game, he is always ready for whatever might come next. He plays hard every play and never stops trying to win. Plus it also helps that George is one the most talented players of all time.

"I just wish I could hit like George." Frank chuckled again. I smiled, too.

"Joe, some of the best advice I ever received was to watch all the great players. Watch Pete Rose, Amos Otis, Reggie Jackson. Each one has something different to teach you, each one plays the game hard, with passion, and with the drive to win each and every night."

The next question was the most important question in my young life. I knew I was a small kid and I was scared that I may never be big enough to play professional baseball. But despite that I just had to know: "How can *I* get great at baseball? How can I get as great as you?"

"Talent helps, but practice is the key, Joe. Practice, practice, practice. Play lots of baseball. That's the most important thing. Practice as often as you can, but what's even more important is to practice correctly. Perfect practice makes you the best player you can be."

That's it? Practice. *All I have to do is practice a lot and do something I love?* That didn't seem like too much to ask of me since I already knew that all I wanted to do was play professional baseball. At least that was the narrative that became my life story.

CHAPTER TWO

LIKE ANY OTHER DAY

Twenty-eight days. Twenty-eight days is how long it was before I'd be back in my house again. My mother thought (and so did I) that when she called to wake me up one morning it wasn't anything other than the start to just another day, like any other day. That's what it was. But not for long.

I had only two things on my mind back then. Football and girls. I wanted to look good for both. In the growing town of Olathe, Kansas, a suburb of Kansas City, Indian Trail Junior High had reopened after the summer break and the air was already crisp in the early hours of September 11, 1984. I was 14, athletic, lean, and strong, but also only 5-foot-6 and 115 pounds. I was in ninth grade, yet I had my future laid out before me like dominos. I was going to play baseball at Arizona State, then play professional baseball. I was going to marry the girl of my dreams. I was going to make a difference in the world. I was going to be a professional baseball player like Frank White, and no one was going to stop or prevent me.

Mom and I had begun our usual morning banter that day when I poked my head out from under warm flannel covers.

"Joe, it's time to get up, sweetie," my mother yelled at me in my bedroom. "Joe, now!"

"*What?* Leave me alone! I'm not ready to get out of bed yet, Mom!"

"Well you better, or you'll be late for the school bus and I'll be damned if I'm going to drive you."

Ah, memories.

Slightly favoring my left knee that was still tender from the football game the previous week, I slid out of bed and considered my wardrobe for the day. I slipped Huey Lewis' 1984 into my Boom Box and sang along, choosing black slacks, Nike shoes and my new shirt. I remember that shirt. It was short sleeved, two-toned, white with red at the shoulders and a black collar on a white body. I struck a few poses in front of the mirror, smiled at myself and thought, Damn, I look good!

While Mom fixed breakfast, I recall radio voices that spoke in the background… President Reagan announced the appointment of two senators as representatives in the United Nations General Assembly scheduled for later in the month…Hurricane Diana continued her path of destruction up the North Carolina coast. But I wasn't interested in politics or the weather. Not then anyway. The only thing of interest that morning was getting out the door before I'd run into my stepfather, Hank. I was still angry with him after the fight we had the week before, so I gobbled my breakfast, gathered my books, and looked over my shoulder as I walked out the door, reminding my mother that I'd see her later.

"Careful!" she warned.

Mom always said that. And I gave it no thought. How careful did a 14-year-old have to be? I was invincible after all. It was like any other day or so I thought until I laid flat on my back on our practice field and heard Coach Largent shout, "Someone call an ambulance now!" And I heard myself say…

"Where are my arms? I can't feel my arms."

CHAPTER THREE

MVP?

The season before the paralyzing football injury that changed my life, we had beaten our rivals Oregon Trail 12-6 and I was the MVP of that game. I had 12 solo tackles and made the game-saving play. I had one of the best moments of my young life. You don't forget a game like that.

It was a cold, blustery Kansas day. I was never a big fan of cold weather games. Every hit or tackle hurt just a little bit more. I was bundled up as much as I could be with a thermal undershirt under my shoulder pads and still be able to function with my equipment and uniform. The game was a defensive struggle. We were winning 12-6 with a minute left on the clock and Oregon Trail was driving to try to score the winning touchdown. They had marched the ball down to our twenty-five yard line, using their bruising running back JR Sanchez. JR and I had a history. We had played baseball together that past summer on the All-Star team. Sanchez was a beast. Imagine a 13-year-old like Sanchez with legs the size of tree trunks and a reputation that he could not be stopped. As Oregon Trail's team lined up, the formation and what I saw in their eyes all said *sweep to our left*. Sweep, a type of offensive play where the quarterback would toss the ball to the running back and he'd run to one side of the field following his line of blockers.

I was responsible for the split-out wide receiver. I don't remember his name, but I remember he was tall and lanky, not as big as Sanchez. Right before the ball was snapped, he kept looking back to our right. I was one of those kids when every time coaches showed something about other teams and every Super Bowl or every anything about football, I watched it. All I did was watch sports in those days. So being a student of the game at such a young age, I wondered. *Why would he keep looking back to the right?* His eyes kept telling me something was up. So I prepared for a sweep back right, not left. As soon as the ball was snapped, the wide receiver took one step towards me like he was going to run to go to a pass. Sanchez, the running back, got the handoff and immediately flipped the ball back to the WR on the reverse and there was no one on the right side to stop him, except me. As I weaved my way through teammates, I came out and there was my man running with the ball, headed for the game-tying touchdown. With a burst of speed, I lunged for him and made the tackle. I also stripped the ball from behind and made the recovery and essentially saved the game. I can still remember one of the older students who watched the game came up to me and said, "Joe, you saved the game with that tackle. You're the MVP." It was intoxicating to be hailed as the savior and the Most Valuable Player in such an important game. My confidence went through the roof and I felt there was nothing I couldn't do.

During my six years of playing football, basically from 8-years-old to 14, I had never missed a game. I was in eighth-grade when we, Indian Trail Junior High, outplayed our rival, Oregon Trail. But entering the ninth-grade season the next year, that streak was broken. I had missed the first game of the season that year because I had twisted and sprained my knee. I was more determined than ever to never let that happen again, but I had to sit out a practice as Coach Largent told me to sit out and rest before the next game when we'd play Oregon Trail again. So I missed a practice, but I dared not tell my stepfather, Hank.

CHAPTER FOUR

THE LAST PRACTICE

At 6-feet-2 and 220 pounds, my stepfather Hank was a big man who didn't tolerate weakness. Missing football practice was weakness in his eyes, or so I thought. After I sat out during the Monday practice, Hank stood poised in the kitchen, waiting for me to get home. He was an intimidating figure with bright red hair and an abundant red mustache and his signature cowboy hat and cowboy boots. Hank was a modern-day cowboy who owned several ranches and a cattle company. He was a cattleman and he did team roping in competition, like a rodeo without bull riding. He was no-nonsense.

"Where were you?" Hank demanded in his throaty drawl, already knowing the answer because he'd gone to the practice and I wasn't there. Coach Largent told me I could sit out the practice with my sprained knee. Then I went to a girl's house.

"Practice," I told Hank, feeling the flush in my face. He did not tolerate bullshit or lies. For Hank, a man's word was his bond.

"Did you practice today?"

"Yes." I lied. It was stupid to lie and I knew it, but still did it anyway. Not very smart.

Furious, in a split second, Hank swung his hand in the air and smacked it across my face as Mom looked on in horror. My hand flew to my stinging cheek. "I hate you!" I yelled as I ran to my room, tears streaming down my reddened cheek. "I hate you. You're not my father!" Being a typical teenager, I meant it at the time, but my anger didn't last as long as my grudges did. Hank was gritty and tough and him slapping me was not the right thing to do, but it was how he was raised.

Next day, I was back in the locker room, getting my pads on before practice and jawing with my teammates about how Marino and the Dolphins had lit up the Redskins in the previous Sunday's game. "I could cover Marc Duper and Mark Clayton. They aren't much bigger than me," I said. Well at least I thought I could in my own head. We would soon be facing our biggest rival Oregon Trail in the next game, three days away. Oregon Trail vs Indian Trail might as well have been Boston vs New York, North Carolina vs Duke, Harvard vs Yale, Kansas vs Missouri. Determined to beat the Oregon Trail Tigers like we did the year before was a big deal for our team and we could feel the pressure of the school on us. On game days, cheerleaders wore their outfits and players wore our jerseys over a shirt and tie. All the kids knew who the football players were. The pressure was from the coaches and we put pressure on ourselves. And sore knee or not, I was going to play. So before game day, I was back at practice. I sprinted out onto the bottle-green field in the humid afternoon air and I replayed my mantra in my head: *Desire*, how bad do I want to win? *Effort*, how much work was I willing to put in? *Focus*, was I willing to not be distracted? *Belief*, did I believe above all else that I could win? I reminded myself of this every time I stepped onto a football field or baseball diamond. Want it more. Work harder than anybody else. Keep my eye on my target. Always believe I can do it no matter what.

Coach Largent had coached for 25 years. We talked a lot and we knew he loved his players, but he tested our limits each day, pushing us to find more strength, more endurance than we knew we had. It'd be after 5:00 when practice was winding down before we'd run the dreaded sprints. We'd practice for two hours, then we'd have to line up and run on the field. If somebody lagged behind, we'd have to do it over. The drill didn't allow any Lollygaggers.

Practice was very intense as we prepared for Oregon Trail. During practice that day, howls of pain ripped through the September air. One of my teammates was on the ground, writhing in pain, his ankle cupped between his hands. Another injury. Coaches know injuries are an expected but unfortunate part of the game. Coaches are trained in handling injuries and our coaches were no different. We all knew the risks of broken bones and sprains and I had learned that lesson the week before.

As I watched my teammate, I thought about my knee injury and the visit with my Orthopedic Specialist came back to me. He was accustomed to more serous injuries and he explained my injury was only a sprain. "Ice it for a few days and give it a rest," he said.

Me? Rest? I laughed to myself. I was smug. *Doesn't he know my team needs me? They had already won the first game of the season without me and we were going to play Oregon Trail next, so rest is not what I even wanted to consider.* Then he said something that at the time I gave no real thought to, but it was actually prophetic:

"Joe, if you don't get bigger, you're going to get seriously hurt."

Whatever, I thought. *I'm big enough. This knee injury is the first time I have ever been hurt, so whatever, Dude.* Like most young people, I was strolling through life with a delusion of invincibility, a not-me-syndrome.

After my teammate was taken to the hospital, we continued to practice with as much intensity as before, but I started feeling more fatigued than usual. I had missed the previous week, so naturally I was not in as good of shape as I would have liked to be. But nothing was going to prevent me from finishing practice with me giving everything I had left in the tank. We'd been scrimmaging the starting defense team versus the second-team offense. I was the left-side cornerback on defense and as the offense snapped the ball, I was initially distracted, laughing about something with first-year Assistant Coach Jeff Meyers. I lost my focus. I don't recall what we were laughing about, but I spun around to get set. Too late. The play was underway. Coach Largent had called for the tight end (an offensive position who mainly blocked but would catch the ball sometimes) to run a pass pattern called a *down and in* (where the tight end runs four yards down the field then makes a 90-degree turn right towards the middle of the field). Coach had designed the play to test me as I later found out, to see if I'd be able to determine what the tight end was doing and if I'd read the play correctly and make the tackle. Basically, he wanted to see if I had paid attention while I was injured with my sprained knee. And I had.

When it came to being prepared, I always paid attention. I never forgot how Frank White described George Brett: *His head is always in the game. He is always ready for whatever may come next.* Remembering that, I worked hard at being the best I could be for every play, everyday. Baseball was my best sport, but football was my favorite to play. I loved the intensity. The tackling. To be able to knock the hell out of a player. The feel of the helmet on my head. I loved it all too much not to pay attention. That day, though, I was getting winded easily and it was a struggle to keep up the pace. But I remember the ball rocketed through the air and the tight end caught it and tucked it away under his arm as I ran towards him to make the tackle. I wanted to explode into it—I tried to explode into it—but my body, tired and sluggish, didn't respond as my mind had told it to. The big tight end, all 6-feet-2, 195 pounds of him bolted toward me. Me, all 5-feet-6, 115 pounds, lowered my head and prepared for the tackle.

Yes, I lowered my head.

I broke the cardinal rule of tackling: *Head up, eyes on your target, lead with your shoulder.* A rule that had been drilled into our skulls time and time again. Yet, instead of looking at the target and using my shoulder to make the tackle, I used my helmet and thrust it into my teammate's thigh like a battering ram.

The tackle snapped my neck down and back on impact. I was hurled backward, flying through the air, weightless, smashing to the ground, spread-eagled. Stunned.

The sky was bright blue, I remember. I laid there for those few seconds still stunned. Then I heard muted mumbles as a team of voices drew closer. *What was happening?* The world was surreal. Muffled. Then it hit me.

I can't move. I can't feel my arms. Where are my arms? I wondered as I gasped for breath. My body was weightless. I laid motionless on the ground. I remember thinking, *My arms are ripped out of my body.* That's what it felt like.

That was my last practice and the last real play of my life. September 11, 1984, a day like any other day until I heard Coach Largent shout, Ambulance!

CHAPTER FIVE
I'M SORRY

"I'm sorry," I whispered, feeling ashamed for causing such a commotion, for failing, for letting my coach down. "I'm sorry, Coach. I know better than that."

I laid on the ground and struggled to breathe. As I gasped for air, thoughts machine-gunned in my head. I tried to call out, Where are my arms? I can't feel my arms, but it only came out like a whisper, as if a pillow had been put over my face. I thought of my teammate who had hurt his ankle earlier in the day and the sound of his painful howls filled my head. I knew this was different. I felt no pain. I wasn't rolling around on the ground screaming in agony like my teammate had. I didn't feel anything. The blue sky was suddenly eclipsed by the hot, sweating forms of my teammates who peered down at me. Their mouths moved, but I couldn't make out what they were saying. Then out of the muffled din I heard Coach Largent yell, "Get back! Get back! Give him some air!" They parted and let him through.

"Hang in there, Joe," Coach said to me. You would think I had a million things to remember, but the mind must have a strange way of coping, because I remember a bead of sweat fell from his brow and dangled from the face mask of my helmet. The sun's rays stretched out behind the coach, his silhouette looming before my eyes. I was confused. No matter what had ever happened, I had always gotten up. I gasped for some breath and uttered as loud as I could, but it only came out as a whisper.

"Where are my arms? I can't feel my arms."

Nobody answered. I sensed movement above me and I was fairly aware of a rumble of voices. Kneeling in close, looking directly into my eyes, Coach said, "A pinched nerve, Joey. That would explain why you can't feel your arms. Now, we want you to try to stay as still as you can. We're going to take care of you. And don't try to move your head, Joe," he warned. As he spoke, Coach Largent had been sticking pins into my legs, but I was completely unaware. And he had been plucking hairs from my legs. Again, I felt nothing. I struggled to breathe like a fish gasping on dry land, slowly taking in each breath, one breath at a time, as if it were my last.

The shrill song of sirens soon pierced the afternoon air, drawing closer as the ambulance drove onto the field. It was at that moment that terror swept over me and hit me like a violent wave crashing, sucking me under. But it wasn't just fear, it was fear laced with confusion. My teammates' faces looked like they were stricken with alarm. The boys made room for paramedics to unload their equipment and begin asking me a series of questions.

"What's your name?"

"Joe," I responded.

"How old are you? Do you know what day of the week it is?"

"I'm 14, and it's Tuesday September 11th."

The questions continued as they covered my face with an oxygen mask and laid the long, rigid stretcher next to my paralyzed body. They carefully braced my neck, preparing me for transport. As I was later to find out, one wrong move could have meant permanent paralysis—or even death. Today as we watch football games on TV, it's natural that when we see a player going down and not moving, our worst fear instantly comes to mind. We say to ourselves, *Please let him be okay. Please get up.* Because not getting up, our fear is coming true. With great care, the medics rolled me onto the board, securing my head by taping it down to the backboard. It was then that I noticed my stepfather Hank standing over to the side. My first thought was, *What is he doing here?* Then I wondered, *How long have I been laying on the field?* I didn't live far away from the school, but when did my coaches call him? The fear was growing. I knew they'd only call my parents if it was serious.

I could see the lines of worry etched onto Hank's face like cracks in a mountainside. He had later told me that while he was standing there watching it all unfold he was thinking: *Why the hell isn't my son getting up? He's a tough boy.* "Just get up," Hank said he repeated to himself, over and over as his panic worsened. "Just get up."

I wondered where my mother was as my limp body went into shock. "I don't care if it takes you an hour to get to the hospital, don't hit any bumps along the way," said a paramedic as he closed the ambulance door. It was then that I closed my eyes for the first time.

When Life Knocks the Hell Out of You

CHAPTER SIX
THE HOSPITALS

M y mind was in another world. Everything had a dream-like quality as I drifted in and out of consciousness, barely aware of the muffled sounds that swirled around me, echoing between the hollow halls and my mind. Somewhere near—or somewhere far off—wheels turning...the harsh clang of metal...a tinny-sounding voice on a PA system. It was a struggle to remain aware as the gurney was pushed urgently across the tiled floors of the emergency room. It was then that I saw her. I saw my mother for the first time. Each one of us in our lifetime have had our mothers look at us in a million different ways. But I had never seen the look on my mom's face that she was giving me at that moment. She looked scared, confused, sad, and angry all at the same time. But mostly she looked at me with loving eyes.

Then I noticed the teammate who had left practice before me was still waiting for his broken ankle to be attended. Our eyes met briefly, but neither of us uttered a word as I was rolled past him.

Hank and my coaches were all in the ER as well but it was my mother's comforting voice that I listened for. She looked rigid, like her muscles had tensed as she stood anxiously beside me, trying to stay near but out of the way. What if her son would never walk again? What if he didn't make it through the night? She watched the nurses and doctors scramble around her son, still bundled in my heavy uniform.

My mother was pretty, so pretty that in the late 1960s, she was a Playboy Bunny, a waitress at the Playboy Club on the top floor ballroom of the Continental Hotel in downtown Kansas City. I wasn't born yet, but I've seen pictures. She was pretty, but she was not a stranger to tragedy. Her parents, Joseph and Willie Jean, had six children, my mom being the eldest and the only daughter with five younger brothers. They were Jerry, Jack, Jeff, Johnny, and Jay. Mom told me their father died of a heart attack before I was born, and she told me what happened with her brothers. I was around and older when her brother Jack died of an aneurism at age 38. Jeff would later commit suicide. He was found with a shot-gun blast to his chest. Years later, Johnny was car-jacked and viciously smashed in the skull with a brick, leaving him with a severe brain injury and in need of constant care from her. Indeed, my mother had seen her share of grief in her lifetime. She had a hard life and, to me, she was as strong as anyone who lived. She would need that tenacity for the several years ahead, as would I.

The hospital attendants swiftly undressed me for X-rays. They maneuvered around me, holding me, turning me, hands and arms working around tubes and monitors, instructing each other with calm, yet urgent voices. But none of them had ever encountered an injured football player with full helmet and pads still on. They were not sure how to remove my helmet without moving my neck at the same time. Fortunately, Coach Largent was there, and he informed them of the best way to remove my helmet.

They first unscrewed the face mask and then popped out the ear pads, which gave more room to stabilize my head and gently slide the helmet off. Next, the shoulder pads were delicately removed. Each move was done with the greatest of caution. If a tiny bone fragment as small as a finger nail clipping was loose within the spinal canal, the fragment could travel and nick the spinal cord, causing permanent damage that could never be reversed, I learned later. So every step of the process was handled with extreme caution. Scissors sliced through my most-prized practice jersey and nimble fingers untied the leg and knee pads. During training camp and before school had started, our coaches informed all of us that if we played exceptional defense, we'd earn a mesh skull and crossbones tear-away jersey. It was like the Nebraska Cornhuskers version of their black shirts on defense. I earned my jersey and it was an honor to be wearing it. So when it was cut away, believe it or not, I was upset over that at the moment. Yes, I was sill 14.

I was prepped for X-rays. Forty-five minutes later, the X-rays told the story that no one wanted to hear. My neck was broken, fractured in two vertebras.

My mother's legs weakened. She could barely stand. But X-rays couldn't tell the whole story. To fully assess the damage done to my neck and spinal cord, I would have to have a CAT scan. Like many hospitals in 1984, Olathe Medical Center wasn't equipped to deal with that type of injury, that level of trauma, so arrangements were quickly underway to transport me to the nearest hospital with a Level One Trauma Center. Level One being highest and staffed with trauma surgeons, including those trained in such specialties as neurosurgery and orthopedic surgery, as well as having highly sophisticated medical diagnostic equipment. That was Shawnee Mission Medical Center, which was 30 minutes away. The nurses cleaned me up and I was prepped to leave, my life hanging by a thread as the swelling increased around my spinal cord with each passing moment.

"Joe has a broken neck," was said aloud by the ER Doctor. Upon hearing those words, my head started to spin, I felt nauseous, and just like that, I threw up, then slipped into unconsciousness.

The next morning, I awoke in Shawnee Mission Hospital's Trauma Center, feeling groggy, struggling to focus, hovering between a drug-induced sleep and wakefulness. I seemed to recall an accident, an ambulance, and I wondered, *Was it a nightmare?* I shook off the web of sleep and began to pry my eyes open and I saw my father, Joe Sr., standing before me at the side of my narrow bed. Oh no! It was not a nightmare. My father had been called. It was real. Terror was with me once again.

My dad had flown in on a red-eye flight from Cleveland and he looked tired, older, than the last time I had seen him.

"How you doing, Son?" Dad asked, barely able to get the words out. When he asked that question, I realized I still could not feel my arms or my legs. My body felt as though it had disappeared and I wasn't able to move it. Salty tears welled up in my eyes and as they streamed down my face, anger filled my heart for the first time as I realized I couldn't even wipe my own tears away. I felt embarrassed and ashamed, and even angry that I was crying in front of my dad.

"It's okay, Son. Everything will be okay. You're okay," my father whispered to me.

My dad was one-hundred percent Sicilian blood and born and raised in Cleveland, Ohio. My mother, Judi, Scot-Irish, was born in Hot Springs, Arkansas, but raised in Olathe, Kansas, a suburb of Kansas City, for most of her life. The two, both strong-willed and stubborn, married shortly after meeting and were constantly at odds with each other, from what I'd been told. I didn't know until she told me that my mother had given up a son for adoption in 1967 and it had left her with terrible guilt and a void in her heart. She had made up her mind that she wanted a chance at having another son, and if she met the right man, Well, look out! She was still single when she and a girlfriend moved to Lawton, a small town in Oklahoma. Fort Sill, an Army base, is where my father was stationed and it was only three miles from Lawton. Both my dad and my mother ended up working at a local bar *The Guys and Dolls*, she a server and he a bartender after he was discharged. Theirs was a passionate affair, full of love and lust from what I've heard. Before they knew it, she was pregnant and he was asking her to marry him.

The union apparently wasn't a happy one from the outset and their home was filled with constant shouting, tension and disagreement.

I'm not wanting to go into the awful and embarrassing details except to say they must have been young and foolish and stubborn. The marriage was over as quick as it had begun, but by then they were living in Cleveland. They divorced and, as far as I know, the custody battles over me were ugly, because two hard-headed people did not want to give up any ground. My mother ultimately won full custody and my dad had visiting rights. Then on Father's Day in 1976, my mother had had enough of dealing with Cleveland. She longed to return home.

She packed me and my sister up, and left for a new/old life in Kansas City. She didn't tell my father we were leaving and she didn't warn him. When he arrived at his usual time to pick me up on that Father's Day, he found an empty home and a note:

Joe

I've taken the kids back to Kansas City. I'm sorry, but I can no longer live without my family, and no longer want to live in Cleveland. We don't belong here. I don't belong here. I am sorry to do this, Joe.

Judi

To say that was not the best Father's Day for my dad was an understatement. His 5-year-old son was gone, snatched away from him without warning. It's not like he could just pick up his cell phone back then and make a call to see where we were. I think he was furious for a long time. But the distance between us never diminished his love for me. I felt it. And he showed it. He always hugged me and told me he loved me and we spoke a lot on the phone.

Then there he was, looking down at me as I lay weeping in a hospital bed, paralyzed from the neck down.

My dad is a strong man and he too had seen his share of hardship. While fighting in Vietnam, he had seen friends killed, bodies shredded by explosives, bullets ripping through muscle and bone.

Yet he was weakened by the sight of me laying helpless in front him. He wanted to wipe my tears away, knowing I was embarrassed by them, but he could only smile down at me, hiding his pain, trying to be the strong father figure he thought I desperately needed at that moment.

Others in the room tried to remain cheerful...*Good morning, Sleepyhead...How did you sleep last night?* as my nurse stood sentinel taking my vital signs. Then in walked Dr. Charles Striebinger, somber and troubled, a furrow creasing his brow. Dr. Striebinger was a brilliant neurosurgeon who looked like he walked straight out of a Ralph Lauren magazine with his silver hair and cowboy boots. Yet if you wanted a doctor with a good bedside manner, he was not your guy. He is and was as dry as they come and he didn't sugar coat anything. He looked around at all who were in the room, my mother, my father and my stepfather, and he said words that still hurt to this day.

"Joe needs to be prepared to use a wheelchair for the rest of his life."

I thought I would throw up again like I had before. Think about it. I couldn't move. I couldn't lean forward. I could only vomit all over myself. This time, I didn't. Instead, I slowly drifted back into sleep and dreamed strange dreams. I was strapped to a metal table in a dark cave, a dark steel cave. Thunderous noise whirled overhead and I was trapped, or was I in a helicopter?

I didn't wake up again until the next morning, thinking about my mom.

CHAPTER SEVEN

A SONG FOR MOM

M y mother walked into a dark house after the long drive home from Shawnee Mission Medical Center, exhausted from the strain, worn out from worry about me. I'm aware of what she went through because pieces of the story were told through the years. That night, Hank flicked on the kitchen light when they came home. My mom wanted to stay in the darkness and shadows but, knowing Hank, she knew it would be silly to ask. She needed to think. Her son's injury would affect all their lives, and certainly her most recent plan to leave Hank. After witnessing Hank hit my face the week before, after years of his stern resolve, she had decided to leave him. Now, how could she? She didn't have a job that would support her and her son and daughter, and she didn't have the emotional fortitude to get through the ordeal of my injury alone. She knew she needed Hank, his strength and support, now more than ever. He was, after all, a strong man, a man who took care of his family. And they had loved each other once. That's what I've been told.

Although my mom had won her battle against cigarettes, she needed one then. She said she remembers that she could almost taste one, almost feel the smoke sweep over her tongue, down her throat, satisfying that strong need. After hearing the warnings on the news from the Surgeon General, she had thought she would never start again. But that night, she needed something to soothe her. She asked Hank if he would be so kind to go get her a pack from the convenient store that was right down the road from where we lived. He said, "Yes. No problem."

As she heard the purr of his engine move out of the driveway, my mother sat alone in her living room, in the darkness she desired, and she began to weep. My sister Guylene was away at college, the University of Kansas, and she didn't yet know about what had happened to me, so the house was quiet except for the radio…My mother told me later that she remembers like it was yesterday sitting in the dark and listening to Lionel Richie's voice sing plaintively in the background. It was filled with sadness and longing, and my mom felt the lyrics from his song….

And I want to tell you so much, I love you…

How could she tell my sister what had happened? How could she say those words? She practiced saying them in her head. "Your brother has had a terrible accident. He broke his neck."

And tell you time and time again, how much I care…

"Joey broke his neck, dear, but he's going to be all right."

Sometimes I feel my heart will overflow.
Hello? I've just got to let you know…

"Joey may never be able to walk again, Guylene. We have to be strong for him."

Are you somewhere feeling lonely. Or is someone loving you…

"Joey had an accident playing football. His neck broke and he's paralyzed from the neck down. But everything will be fine."

Tell me how to win your heart. For I haven't got a clue.
But let me start by saying, I love you

She couldn't do it. She couldn't tell Guylene. She couldn't make the words sound right. How could she when she could hardly believe herself? Whimpers became heavy sobs. Tears became burning torrents. She held her hand on her heart like it would escape from her chest and she leaned her head up to the heavens."God! Please! Please! Please help my son. I don't know what we will do if he can't walk. Please help him. I need you."

Hello…Is it me You're looking for?

My mom was tired. She said she had had enough that night. As soon as Hank got home with her cigarettes she was going to smoke one, or two, maybe the pack, and then go to bed. For she had to get up early the next morning and be there for her son.

Are you somewhere feeling lonely. Is someone loving you?

CHAPTER EIGHT

ALONE

O nly a boy alone in the darkness in a hospital bed could know what that feels like--to be that boy, alone at night, alone when the first instances of feeling start to rip through one's broken neck, down into the shoulders, squeezing the muscles behind the ears and searing throughout every part that can feel anything at all. So it was, as my body began to recover sensation, my brain recognized it as pain. The brain began to get those messages through my bruised spinal cord pathways and more pain was released. It was the most agonizing feeling I had ever felt in my young life. It reminded me of growing pains, only magnified about 100 times.

"Nurse?" I would try to call out. "Nurse? Hello, is anyone there? Please, can anyone hear me?"

The sound of my voice was weak, barely a scratchy whisper escaped and melted into the sterile air. Instinctively, I tried to reach for the buzzer with my paralyzed arms, only to be reminded that I couldn't move them.

"Nurse?!" Please someone come in my room, I am hurting so bad. Please, anyone. Can anyone hear me?"

Tears began to stream down my face as the reality of my situation began to sink in deeper. I was sad, angry, frustrated and alone.

Alone. No one to talk to. No one to ask for help. All alone. Helpless and frightened. My eyes continued to well up and burn as salty tears slid from the corners of my eyes and trailed down the side of my face, pooling uncomfortably in my ears or down my neck. I couldn't wipe them away. *I can't move!* I wanted to scream. *Where is everybody?*

The nights lasted too long. Alone, one night after another. In pain. In tears. Filled with anger. And across town, my mother would cry herself to sleep, wondering if I was okay. Hoping—believing—that I was fast asleep. If you would ever ask me what the worst part of the hospital was, I'd simply say, the nights. Being alone and in pain with no one there to comfort me or help me. Then to finally cry myself to sleep, only to have a nurse come in my room and wake me up to check my vitals. Yes, nights were the very worst.

CHAPTER NINE
HALO

My mind was playing tricks on me. After drifting in and out of sleep throughout the first night in the Pediatric Ward of the Shawnee Mission Medical Center, I faintly recalled dreaming about the mind-numbing words I had heard the day before…broken neck. It couldn't be true. They must have made a mistake. They had to make a mistake, had to have read the wrong X-rays. They were talking about someone else. Yes, that's it. They made a mistake.

"Joe, Joe, wake up please."

I awoke to the room already full of people: My father, mother, Hank, Dr. Striebinger, and a few nurses and techs to boot. I didn't know why they were all in my room. Regardless, there was no amount of preparing me for what was about to come.

It was September 13, 1984 and on that day Indian Trail Junior High was to play our dreaded rival, Oregon Trail. That was one of the first things that came to my mind. The medical staff decided that day I would sit up for the first time. For the last two days, I mainly slept and if I did wake up, I couldn't get up if I wanted to. I had been placed in traction with the Gardner-Wells Traction. Weights helped to relieve the pressure on the bones. I had no idea the Gardner-Wells Traction had been screwed into my skull. I was asleep for that. The Gardner-Wells Traction was not fun and did not allow me to sit up in it anyway.

As the nurses and doctor gently maneuvered me and adjusted the bed, all the blood rushed into my brain and my head went into a nauseous spin. I looked at my mom and seeing her there gave me a fleeting sense of comfort and safety. Even if it was only for a moment, just having her there helped me. My mom was a beautiful woman, but not on that day. She looked chalky and gaunt, as though she had been awake all night, crying. And indeed, she had been. Worry and fear made themselves at home on her face and puffy eyes peered out from pale skin. I was the one injured, but I think my mother was the one who was most wounded those first nights.

"Could I speak to you all out in the hallway for a moment?" I overheard someone ask. It was the Neurologist Dr. Striebinger. My parents slipped quietly out of the room, their stomachs probably in tight knots. I was later told of the conversation Dr. Striebinger had with my family: "I need to discuss the diagnosis and treatment for Joe's injury. As you know, the fourth- and fifth-cervical vertebrae have been fractured," he said, putting the X-ray on a whiteboard and circling the area with his finger. But the news got worse. "The scans also revealed a compression of the fifth vertebra and a herniation of the seventh." What did this mean? Fracture? Compression? Herniation? I'm sure nausea churned in my mother's gut.

"The good news is that no bone fragments had entered his spinal cord."

Good news was all my mom, Hank and my dad said they heard. But what did it mean that "No bone fragments had entered into his spinal cord." Then why is he paralyzed my family wanted to know. Dr. Striebinger recognized the glazed eyes and pinched look on their faces. He had seen it many times and he paused for a moment to let the news sink in. Then he went on to explain more about my condition:

"When a spinal cord is injured, it swells for several hours, sometimes days, and Joe's swelling had compressed inside of the cord, leaving a severe spinal cord bruise. If any bone fragments, even as small as a finger nail clipping had entered into the spinal cord, or even had nicked it in any way, there would be no hope for a full recovery. The fact that Joe has a severe spinal cord bruise could still mean total paralysis, but because no bone fragment had entered into his spinal cord, there is still a chance that he could possibly get some movement back.

"But let me be very clear. Most likely, Joe will need to be prepared to use a wheelchair for the rest his life.

"There are no two spinal cord injuries that are identical. The spinal cord has over 150 million nerve fibers, so predicting precise results about return of function is impossible," he explained. "Sometimes, surgery is needed, particularly for spinal cord or nerve injuries. Fusing the neck would involve delicate surgery in which the neck vertebrae can either be removed or joined using bone from somewhere in the body, restricting motion between the vertebrae." The doctor explained the procedure using a welding analogy.

"Bone grafts are placed around the spine and 'welded' to it. Over several months, if all goes well, the body heals the grafts. But sometimes, even with the surgery, the odds of recovery are not good. Mr. Rhea, Mr. and Mrs. Walton, you and the whole family, must know—must be prepared—as I stated earlier, Joe could spend the rest of his life in a wheelchair. But the surgery is not our only option. Because no bone fragments were detected in his spinal column, Joe could bypass surgery that would 'fuse' his neck, if you all so choose."

This was a no-brainer for them. My mother told me they were relieved to have another alternative: The Halo. Dr. Striebinger came in the room to explain it to me and everyone else. I was no angel...I knew I was no contender for a Halo. Especially not later in life. (Foreshadowing.)

"So, what is it?" I asked reluctantly, because it didn't sound like it could be any fun at all.

"Well, this is a round, metal traction device, Joe. It's designed to hold your head perfectly still while you are wearing it. First, we'll have to shave a little of your head to get started."

"You have to do WHAT!?" The idea of having my head shaved for any reason wasn't even imaginable. My hair was my identity. It was what the girls loved to run their fingers through. My brown curly locks of hair.

"Joe, Joe, snap out of it. Pay attention," said mom, obviously noticing me daydreaming.

"Do you really have to shave my hair? I asked. "Why? What are you going to do?" As soon as I asked the question, I caught sight of the pointed screws lying on the tray next to my bed. *They're going to drill holes in my head? You have got to be kidding me?* Just a few days before, I was a typical teen concerned about my appearance, my clothes and how I looked to the girls.

"Joe, we have to shave your head because we are going to insert these four steel screws into your skull. Attached to this wool vest you see, it will hold your head in place, allowing your vertebrae the best opportunity to heal naturally."

Whatever man! Do what you gotta do. Get on with it, I thought, having no idea what was actually in store for me.

Once the decision to wear the Halo was made, no time was wasted in the preparation. As I eyed the needles lined up on the stainless steel tray beside my bed, two nurses shaved my head in the two spots where the back screws were to be inserted. One of the nurses picked up a needle and advised me: "This will numb the area, Joey. So you won't feel anything." Perhaps not afterward, but I certainly felt those needles, all four of them being stabbed into my skull. *Four fucking shots,*I thought. It was something from a sci-fi movie and each one hurt more than the last. In case you wonder if a 14-year-old boy really did cuss, the answer is yes, I did, especially when things hurt that bad. I didn't cuss out loud in front of my parents and adults, but inside my head, it was brutal. No shit!

I suffered through that pain, but nothing could prepare me for the sound of hearing my own skull cracking, the sharp violent crackles, like teeth grinding, reverberating loudly in my head. Despite the anesthetic, I felt as though my head was in a vice grip. The pressure made me feel weak and nauseous. The nurses slid the wool-layered, plastic body vest over me. It had four metal bars, two in front, two in back, that came up around my skull. Five other medical staffers were helping Dr. Striebinger hold my body in place and put a protective collar around my neck to keep my head as still as possible. As they pulled out the Halo and Dr. Striebinger grabbed the hand crank used to put the screws in place, I became dizzy with fear and panic.

A war image popped into my mind. I was a soldier on a battle field. *I'm a prisoner of war,* I told myself. *And this is how they are going to torture me. Don't give in! You have to be strong. Stronger than them.* This was the only way I knew how to cope, preparing as if I were in battle, determined not to give in, not to cry, but to be a brave and strong soldier, like my dad. Then they inserted the screws. My body trembled in pain as the calm voices of nurses tried to soothe me. "It's okay, Joey. It's all right, sweetheart." One tear escaped and trickled down the side of my face and angered me.

Crack, crack, crack! The pressure and pain mounted with each turn of the hand crank.

After the last screw was secured and I had regained some composure, I thought about my football team and the game that they had been preparing to play that night against our arch rivals. Football was still on my mind. I hoped our team was ready.

"Please hurry up," I urged. "I need to get to the game. I want to be there for my team."

Nervous laughs escaped from those around me, but the truth of my situation hung heavily in the air, and I was sensitive to the change of mood, the heavy silence, and the diverted eyes. I looked right at Dr. Striebinger, as serious as a 14-year-old boy could be, my eyes hopeful, my heart afraid. An eternity passed within the second it took for the doctor to answer my question:

"Will I be able to play football or baseball again?"

"No."

Just like that. NO!

I could feel tears stream down my face as the word echoed through my mind, *No, no, no... What do you mean, no!? How can you say that to me? It's not true! You're lying.*

But he was right. I would never play football again. But nothing he said at that moment was going to convince me otherwise. Not even the fact I still hadn't moved in two days.

Dr. Striebinger knew I needed to focus on smaller goals than playing sports. According to him, it would be nothing short of a miracle if I played football or baseball again. If I even walked again, I would need patience and hard work if even that were to be accomplished. I couldn't imagine my life without sports. Walking may have been the goal for someone else in my position, but the bar for my ambition was set much higher. To hear that I would never play football or baseball again hit me with a new feeling, and one I had never known before: *Despair.*

Despair is the feeling of hopelessness. So for a competitive young athlete—the invincible Joe Rhea—the All-Star—despair would be beaten down and subdued with drive, passion, confidence, will—winning. This was the biggest game of my life and at that moment I made the most important decision of my life. I decided, *This doctor is wrong. And I am going to do everything I can to prove it. I will be the one to play football or baseball again. Mark my words...*

Later that day, Dr. Striebringer filled out his report: *Patient became nauseous after the insertion of the screws within the skull. Boy has tremendous drive and spirit. Just what he will need.*

CHAPTER TEN

WHY YOU GOT SCREWS IN
YOUR BRAIN?

Bob Meredith, the physical therapist assigned to my case, took an elevator up to the Pediatric Unit, probably knowing this would be one of his sadder cases: a 14-year-old boy, a quadriplegic in full Halo traction. He had read the pathology reports. The nerve roots of C3, C4 and C5 all contribute fibers to the Phrenic nerve which assists the diaphragm and is responsible for respiration. He knew I would have difficulty breathing. He knew this athletic young boy would have trouble accepting his new life.

My room was crowded with personnel and my family whose faces betrayed their fear and concern. Bob would have expected this, but not expect the total lack of concern on the face of his young patient who could barely speak beyond a whisper. *He's confident, perhaps even a little brassy* is what Bob might have thought to himself as he shook hands with my family and made his introduction. I was lying on the bed, smiling, trying to talk, as though I didn't, in fact, have screws in my skull—as though I weren't pinned to a maze of metal, hooked up to monitors, a prisoner in my bed. Masking my fear or being in denial—Bob had seen this type of behavior before. Or was it that I didn't know and hadn't been fully informed that I might never walk again or use my arms. There was no time to waste.

Bob began therapy for both my physical and emotional well-being immediately. Even as the nurses were making their hourly check on my vital signs, Bob began his sessions, starting with a range of motion exercises. He moved my arms in circles, up, and down. Then he moved my legs, pulled and stretched. I couldn't feel a thing and I felt helpless. Silly.

"When will I be able to move my arms by myself?" I asked.

"That might not ever happen, Joe," he said calmly, looking me straight in the eyes. But I didn't believe him. Failure was not in my vocabulary.

The small amount of weight I once had on my body had begun to fall away and within three short weeks, I lost 30 pounds, my frame a tiny, bony version of my former nimble and limbered body. *I look like a child in a concentration camp,* I thought. Little did my therapist know how I was filled with images of war and battle, torture and strength, just to cope. Some nights I was in a POW camp and being paralyzed was a form of torture. I felt I had to be mentally strong and never be broken or I'd let my country down. I could not let "them" break my spirit.

I remained optimistic and determined. Unshakable. But inside, especially alone at night in the dark confines of my hospital room, fear and anger drifted in. I thought about God. I didn't really know God. Both my grandmothers seemed to know Him quite well. My father's mother was Roman Catholic and every time they drove by a church she made the sign of the cross and muttered a quick prayer, just like some professional players did when they took to bat. My maternal grandmother, Grandma Jean, was raised by a Southern Baptist, so religion was all around me and I had heard plenty about God. Over the last few days, lots of people had mentioned Him and thought He could help. Someone even brought a Bible to the hospital as a gift, but it lay there, unopened, for I couldn't flip the pages even if I wanted to. Just the same, I thought I'd give God a try.

"Please God, make me better."

Nothing happened. I tried again.

"God. Are you listening? Please make me better now."

Nothing.

But I was an athlete—and although I didn't know what God was capable of, I felt sure I knew my own capabilities. I worked with Bob and I used Rocky Balboa as an inspiration. The *Rocky* movies were very important in my young life. I wanted to triumph like Rocky did and I often fell asleep believing the next day would be the one—the one where I walked.

"When can I move my legs on my own?" I continued to ask Bob each time we met.

"Joe, this might be it for you. This might be all we get," Bob explained each day, but regardless of the grim outcome and the limits I'd have to learn to live with, Bob treated me as if he had hope. Daily, he rubbed my legs and arms with various types of objects, all with different textures, hoping to stimulate sensory receptors. But even with the therapy, my small body continued to deteriorate. Within weeks, every muscle atrophied. It was a sad sight for my family to see and I became more and more self-conscious. Being a normal 14-year-old kid, I had enough worries about my appearance and had felt awkward enough about my changing body, but being in a wasting condition in a metal contraption was almost unbearable to my psyche.

Bob was also affected by me, the more time he spent with me. He didn't say it out loud, but I felt I knew his thoughts and as a parent, he'd ask himself: *Will I ever let my kids play football? Is it worth it?* Looking back, I'm sure Bob knew that no matter how far I came along in my recovery, there would be lifetime deficits and a life filled with pain.

Many nights, sad and sedated, tired of watching reruns of *Beverly Hillbillies* on TV, I stared at my lifeless limbs and begged, pleaded with them to move. They did not. I'd envision my fingers moving, my hands, my legs, but they did not. I closed my eyes and pretended I was standing, walking—but I couldn't. I asked God, begged God, to just let me raise an arm in the air. Nothing happened. Nothing moved. God never answered. God simply was never there.

Lonesome nights continued, one into another, then one night something unexpected happened. Agonizing pain began to pummel my body. I was beginning to regain feeling, and although it was a good sign, it was a painful way to progress. Then it happened! My left leg moved. It was a small movement, but a movement…the opportunity that I was waiting for and begging for and now I had it and the the pain came with good news. I was finally able to be positioned in a wheelchair. But though I was improving, no one would overestimate the implications and the mood remained dark—even the very room in which I was a prisoner each night took on menacing shadows. But one day, a ray of sunshine crept into my room.

Slid into my room, to be exact.

I had just been positioned in my wheelchair, my parents and family members standing around me with mixed emotions, probably worrying and praying that the wheelchair would only be temporary. That's when a small and fragile 4-year-old boy came sliding into my room on his knees. He scooted nonchalantly between the forest of adults and came to a full stop in front of me. The room became silent and for a moment the boy stared blankly at the Halo that was screwed into my skull. Then his eyes twinkled. His pink lips opened slightly as his countenance brightened.

He said, "What you got in your bawains?"

"What?" I asked.

"What you got in your bawains?" He wanted to know.

"Oh! Screws."

"What you got scwuws in your bawains for?"

Delicious laughter erupted from me and everyone. The boy with no kneecaps delighted the boy with screws in his brains.

In one moment, the feeling in the room went from despair to joy and I learned a great lesson from a child. Even when life is beating you down, life can find a way to remind you how precious it can be and how moments of joy can slip their way into moments of anguish.

CHAPTER ELEVEN

WHERE IT ALL BEGAN

Behind my house there was a baseball diamond which belonged to my elementary school. One summer day when I was only 7-years-old, I remember I sat in my backyard amid overgrown grass and muddied Tonka trucks, watching older boys play their game, listening to them play baseball and yell at each other. I longed to play, to be a part of the group, to show them what I could do. Then suddenly, the crack of the bat on the ball! A small white speck flew through the summer sky, sailing toward me, landing with a thud nearby.

This was my moment! I raced to pick up the ball and mustering all my strength, fired it all the way to home plate. It was like it was on a rope.

"Geez, look at how far he threw that!," a boy yelled. I beamed. The big kids were talking about me and my great arm!

Then there was the time I wasn't much older when Frank White visited our house and told me the simple secret to his greatness: *Practice.* Remembering that night is like a daydream. I can hear my mother's voice, reminding me it was time for my Cub Scout meeting—an outing I usually loved attending and one I wouldn't dare miss. But how often did a boy get to spend time with his favorite baseball player, Frank White? I didn't want my time with Frank to end. As Frank stood up to prepare to leave for the evening, I think he saw the look on my face and he uttered the sweetest words I had ever heard.

"How about if I go to the Cub Scout meeting with you? Think the other Cub Scouts would mind if I tagged along?"

"Mind?" I shouted, leaping into the air letting out a huge whelp. I didn't know it yet, but my life would never be the same.

We walked into the school gym, one by one, and heads turned toward the door—to see Frank White and me beaming beside him, holding his hand. Voices grew louder and louder as the boys, each dressed identical in their blue uniforms and yellow scarves began to swarm us as if we were handing out Wonka Bars with a golden ticket. The air was electric. I had never felt so alive. And that was a defining moment in my life—one that would influence my life forever. It was at that moment that I knew, truly knew, what I wanted to be and who I wanted to be like: Frank White, humble and charming. He set off a yearning in me—a yearning to make people feel the way Frank White had made those boys feel, had made me and my mother feel. I wanted that charisma and that energy. I wanted to be able to walk into a room as Frank had and have that kind of effect. It was powerful and intoxicating and life changing. In that one instance I had known what I wanted to do with my life. I wanted to play baseball, to be a professional athlete and yes, be like Frank.

After meeting Frank, sports became an obsession for me. I watched every sport I could, soaking up everything it could teach me. I was learning about teamwork, about attitude and about what it was to be a sports hero. In 1979, ESPN hit the airwaves and I was hooked. It was the greatest use of television I had ever seen! Sports 24 hours a day! So what if half the day was filled with billiards, Australian Rules Football and Equestrian, ESPN Sports Center had it going on and this 9-year-old was hooked. I bought the Kool-aid and bought it big time. The way the commentators spoke enthusiastically about the determination of athletes...how they glorified the heart and the courage it took to struggle to the big time. I was your typical, all-American boy, who after watching Sports Center every night, knew that I was going to become a professional athlete. It was no pipe dream. From the first moment I began playing sports, it was apparent that I had a gift—agility and balance, strength and hand-eye coordination. As others put it, "God given talent."

More importantly, when it came to having passion and drive to be the best, I felt I was a man among boys. I was driven to win. I wanted to be unsurpassed, nothing less than the greatest. I wanted people to look at me with admiration, respect, awe and reverence. I wanted everyone to think that I, Joe Rhea, was the best baseball player ever. I was determined to prove it. I was going to show the world that I was indeed as good as I thought I was. I wanted to be on ESPN.

Right or wrong, the drive to be the best was burned into my heart and mind. I played every sport I could, and even though other sports were hobbies, baseball was my future. By the time I was eleven, I had made a name for myself in our small town. Each year I played, my reputation grew. "Did you all see that Joe Rhea last night? Kid has a cannon for an arm." That kind of thing.

Although I was usually the youngest, smallest and shortest of my peers, I never let that stop me or slow me down. If anything, it fueled my drive even more. Of course, I understand now that I had the Napoleon Complex (or "short man-syndrome," a pejorative term describing a psychological condition said to exist in both men or women of short stature). Named for Napoleon, the first Emperor of France, the Napoleonic Complex is characterized by overly-aggressive or domineering social behavior and the implication that such behavior is compensatory for the subject's stature. The term is also used generally to describe people who are driven by a perceived handicap to overcompensate in other aspects of their lives. Even though I never said anything outwardly, inside I hated being the shortest and smallest. I knew that if I only had more size, I could be that much better. Despite my size, I was the kid that the coaches wanted to recruit to their teams. I made many friends through sports and I was the object of more than a few crushes, with my dark wavy hair and huge smile. Okay, maybe I made that part up, but I'd like to think I was the object of many girls' affection.

In the summer of 1982, I was playing for a crosstown team called *Mike Dougan's Seed and Sod*. We were in the 11- and 12-year old division (Majors) and I had been named starting shortstop from day one. My play on the diamond spoke for itself. Because shortstop is an important position, I was also thrust into a leadership role, even though I was the smallest and the youngest. And I loved it. I loved the feeling that older boys were coming to me to ask what to do in the practice drill called "Situation." It was during this drill, when I first heard the name Jimmy Watkins, aka Jimbo. I may have thought of myself as the best player in the town of Olathe, but there was someone better than me. He was a 12-year-old boy, Jimmy "Jimbo" Watkins. Put into perspective, Jimmy Watkins eventually signed a full-ride scholarship to play both football and baseball at Arizona State University. Yeah, man. He was good, but no matter who he was, I was not about to back down.

It was a great season and I had proved myself an important part of the team. But I had yet to prove myself against Jimbo Watkins and, according to almost all the people in town who attended any baseball game, Jimmy was the standard. Then the time had come. It happened on an early summer evening in 1982: Jimmy Watkins' team was scheduled to play against my team *Mike Dougan's Seed and Sod*. It was all I could think about the days before the game. All these thoughts raced through my head: *Is Jimbo really that good? What was I going to expect when I faced him? Had he heard of me?*

I can remember like it was yesterday when one of my coaches said, "Oh, great. Watkins is pitching. You boys better be ready to bat as soon as you step to the plate. This boy throws heat, all fastballs. Get your bats off your shoulders." In the first inning, as Jimbo took the mound, Coach reminded us one more time that Jimbo was the sharpest player in the league, so we had better be at our best. "Nine fastballs. That's what you're going to see. Nine fastballs," Coach said. Jimmy had a title that I coveted: The best player in the league. I felt as though I had been challenged personally—and no Jimmy Watkins' fastball was going to get past me.

My first two teammates struck out at bat on three straight fastballs and Coach's words seemed prophetic. So I got ready. I mindlessly made the sign of the cross, imitating what I had seen so many kids do. I was surrounded by religious symbolism, but I had never really questioned the gesture or even tried to understand it. (The questioning came later.) I strode confidently at bat, got into position, dug my cleats in, held my hand high in the air to signal to the ump that I was not yet set. Then, as I dropped my hand, Jimmy wound up and threw his screaming fastball which sped over the plate.

"Strike one!"

A mixture of moans and cheers erupted from the stands. All eyes were on Jimmy and I felt small flutters in my stomach as I remembered Frank White and what he said about facing Goose Gossage. "If you time the pitch just right, you'll hit it a long way." So I stepped into the box and waited for the next fastball, my eyes piercing toward the mound. As Jimmy reared back to throw, I watched the ball release from his fingers and rocket toward me, straight down the middle of the plate. But this time, everything seemed slower and the ball looked huge. I started my swing, putting all my power into it, timing it perfectly and I watched the ball fly off my bat as it ripped over the shortstop's head on a line drive, going all the way to the fence. I sprinted from home and raced around the bases, digging as hard as I could, cutting the angles around the bases to shorten my distance, if only by a little. Then diving head first into third as the fans erupted and jumped out of their seats and my teammates screamed with joy. I slid into third base.

"Safe!"

I was intoxicated with adrenalin and pride. *I, Joe Rhea, got a hit off the great Jimmy Watkins.* I dusted the dirt off my uniform and looked over at Jimmy and he was looking at me. I gave him a little smile and a quick nod, and Jimmy smiled right back at me. me. *He had heard about Joe Rhea and encountered an opponent he could respect.* This was the narrative playing in my head, of course. If it were true I didn't know it and honestly, I didn't care. I had done something my coaches and teammates and fans said could not be done, and I was going to soak up the moment.

The next pitch, Jimmy threw into the dirt and I stole home, sliding right under his tag, scoring a run, and putting us on top, if only briefly. The following inning, it was Jimmy who came up to bat with two outs in the inning. He was an intelligent player and he often hit ground balls then used his blazing speed to beat out the grounders for an infield hit (much like the 2014 Kansas City Royals club, who led the major leagues in infield hits). I was shortstop and hoping he would hit me a ground ball! I wanted so badly to be the one to gun him down. As he walked up to the batter's box, I kept saying to myself, *Hit it to me, hit it to me, please hit it to me.*

As hoped, Watkins hit the ball low into the dirt to my right side and in a split second, I scooped it up by back-handing the ball, and I threw a strike to the first baseman.

"Out!"

The crowd erupted once again and my teammates sprinted around me, giving high-fives and slapping me on the back. I had done it. I had thrown out the great Jimbo Watkins, the best player in our division. *Or was he the second best player?* I was starting to believe in my ability.

While teammates beamed, I saw my mom as she stood in the stands with pride, quietly smiling and clapping her hands, looking at her son with her beautiful green and hazel eyes. I knew she was proud, but the one person whose opinion meant the most was that of my stepfather, Hank. I always wanted desperately to please him and have him think highly of me. This approval I constantly sought was withheld and I tried so hard to get it, it nearly broke me down.

At the end of that 1982 season, I was playing my last game of summer ball when Coach Norton approached me with the news that I had been selected for the All-Star team. My head was in the clouds for a few minutes as I recalled Frank White's words to me: "Practice. Play lots of baseball. To be the best, you got to play with the best." Now I was considered one of the best, and I had never felt better in my young life. I was an All-Star and couldn't wait to tell Mom and Hank.

By the end of the season, I had nearly a .480 batting average, made few errors as shortstop and had the most defensive assists. Joining the All-Star team was something I was once again eager to prove that I belonged. Oh, and yes. I was again the smallest player on the team, besides Scottie Green who was about the same size. The All-Star tournament took place in Spring Hill, Kansas. It was one of the greatest experiences of my life. We played something like eight games in two days, and we won the tournament. The last day of the tournament, I was playing out of my mind at shortstop. Anything and everything that was hit my way, I gobbled up and threw out the runner or made the stop on the line drive. Three games in a row, I recorded the last out on defense. I was in *the Zone*. It felt good, too. After we won the last game and the tourney, I remember my Coach coming over to me and saying, "Joey I can't remember anyone ever playing shortstop better than you played it this weekend." I was beaming with pride! The trophy was presented to our team for winning the tournament and I heard the host announcer say we still have to reward the most valuable player. It never crossed my mind that I would be named MVP. So when I was announced as Most Valuable Player, it was a huge surprise. I still have that trophy to this day. My dream of being the best was coming to fruition and I loved it.

The next day for the very first time, right under a story about the St. Louis Cardinals moving into first place, was my name, printed in the headline of *Olathe Daily News,* our hometown paper. **All-Stars Win Spring Hill Tournament. Joe Rhea is MVP.**

Hell, yeah!!

Over the next two years, my baseball career continually improved and each year only confirmed what I already felt was true: I was destined for the major leagues. I was on my way to becoming a professional baseball player and imagined being like Frank White every time I stepped onto the field. But more importantly, my athletic endeavors and accomplishments had built a foundation of belief within me and an inner strength that would prove vital to my future. I believed in myself and knew that I could accomplish whatever I set my mind to do. *It's all about the mind,* Frank had told me. *It's all about the mind.*

This belief, this attitude proved to be essential when in the years to come, I would be confronted with my greatest challenges yet.

CHAPTER TWELVE

THE FIRE WITHIN

While still in the hospital, my brain was receiving messages from my body and I had regained some small use of my legs. Bob began more advanced therapy. First, Bob made a concerted effort to get to know me...to understand what made me tick. Mostly, he talked to me about sports, gaining my trust. We started to work on standing and transferring from bed to wheelchair, wheelchair to mat and more. As a physical therapist, there were two fundamental principles Bob followed. The first—don't do anything for the patients that they can do for themselves. And the second—push them, challenge them before backing off to let them succeed. So Bob challenged me. He pushed me as much as I wanted to be pushed.

In record time, I was able to take my first steps with the parallel bars. "It's a miracle," I heard a nurse say. I didn't know if that were true, but I hoped if it were, if God had intervened and had actually caused a miracle, then God would also help the kid in the next room with the amputated leg—and my little friend with no kneecaps.

"When will I move my legs like I used to?" I continued to ask. Bob's familiar response followed: "This may be all the return you get, Joe." I had lost the muscle strength I'd built up over the years and would have to rebuild my entire body but I hadn't lost my determination.

"I'll be playing baseball again, you'll see," I told Bob. But I couldn't have been more wrong.

The day Bob brought in a beach ball to work on my hand-eye coordination, I thought that was childish. I felt silly working with a large inflated yellow and blue ball, but I trusted Bob. Sitting a short distance away from him, Bob gently lobbed the ball. It floated through the air toward me, coming directly at me—but I couldn't catch it. And when Bob placed it in my skinny hands, I couldn't throw it. My heart sank. I got angry with the game and didn't want to play anymore. Bob had pushed too hard, too soon and threatened my dreams. And as the sessions continued, twice a day, five days a week, my personality had begun to change. I wasn't the carefree boy Bob had met that first day. What was going on inside my head was complex. Breaking my neck and suffering paralysis, was a tremendous equalizer to my ego. It was humbling to be knocked down so suddenly, so shockingly. But without that ego, I may never have gotten back up again. Looking back at the heartache, my ego was both a blessing and a curse, even though it would be many years before I felt the blessings. At the time, my ego ensured that I'd give my all to recover, but it also ensured I'd never be satisfied with anything less than perfection.

Brave and idealistic thoughts from a young boy, a boy who wanted to be like Frank White lodged in my mind: *I'll be a legend. The whole world of sports will one day know who Joe Rhea is. I'll work harder than anyone can imagine,* I promised myself. But after the session with the beach ball, an anger began to burn within me, an anger which grew every day, every minute…

CHAPTER THIRTEEN
KID IN THE CAGE

After twenty-eight days as a patient, the hospital had done all they could for me. Now it was up to me and the physical therapy Bob and I had done. I was taken home, still trapped in a metal cage, still partially paralyzed. I'm right-handed, but I had some motion in my left arm. The brace that had been drilled into my skull was called a Halo. But it was not a Halo. It was a cage.

When I looked in the mirror, I'd think of an historical picture of a slave sitting there and he has a collar around his neck. Have you ever seen that image? He was trapped. I felt trapped, too. In a cage.

My mother collected cards and pictures sent from the school and from friends and family. Mom said she had prayed to God that her son would finally be home with her again. She'd no longer have to feel that she had abandoned me, alone in a hospital room, night after night. *Maybe the house won't seem so lonely to her*, I thought. *Maybe Mom can get a good night's sleep again.*

I never slept well.

I was propped up with the cage on my head and I couldn't sleep on my stomach or side because I was still partially paralyzed. I slept like a vampire prevented from the norm, unable to sleep. But I went back to school. My parents believed if I could sit at a desk and walk and use my one good arm, I could go to school and be like the other kids. But I wasn't like them. In fact, I was somewhat of a celebrity when I first returned to ninth grade. There was no sense in trying to look inconspicuous. I was the kid in the cage. Thankfully, I was never one to shy away from attention as I had thrived on it during my years excelling at sports. To my gym coach and to everyone's surprise, I didn't sit out of gym class. The first week back, burdened with the awkward Halo atop my head and steel bars on my body, I ran laps around the gym with the other kids. I had the one arm that worked, so I swung it to propel myself as my legs, weak and wobbly, strained under my weight. I was competitive as ever and would not be left out.

"If I hadn't broken my neck, I'd race you around the gym," I'd say to the other kids. "You wait till I'm better," I'd warn them, as if believing it would be true. My teachers said they were amazed by my spirit, and not knowing much about spinal injuries, they also believed I would one day run laps around the other kids, as I had done before.

Aside from sports, there was one other thing I obsessed about. Girls.

I had my share of girlfriends before the accident. Girls who came out to watch me play…girls who giggled as they passed me in the hall…girls who sent notes…girls who cried and sobbed and hugged each other when they heard the news about my injury. Im not ashamed to say I'm a hopeless romantic. Even at age 14, I was always on the lookout for the girl of my dreams. I thought, *My athletic status draws girls to me.* And I was right. But after the injury, I feared, *No girls will like me. Who could like the scrawny kid in the cage? The boy with screws in his brain? The skinny bag of bones that can barely make it around the school gym?* I would soon find out.

Indian Trail Junior High was holding a dance and Mom said her heart skipped up to her throat when I asked permission to go. She knew how I stood out, knew how cruel kids could be, and I think she worried, A*nything could happen to him at a dance—with all those reckless kids, all that noise, all those people moving about, jumping around in the dark.*

"You have to let him go," Hank drawled, shaking his head. "We talked about this, Judi," he said, calling out from the next room in what my mom said was his King's chair. "He needs to move on. Best thing for him. Be a normal kid."

Mom had three days to find something I could wear—something to fit over my traction bars. In the past month, Mom had taken all my clothes to a tailor to have them altered. Velcro, the "miracle fabric of the eighties," came in handy and I had a new shirt, sort of a sweat shirt, something casual to wear to the Friday night dance. Courage won over trepidation, and I entered the gymnasium doors.

Kenny Loggins' *Footloose* blared from large speakers perched on the stage. As the disco strobe light scattered diamonds across the gym walls, I got up the nerve to ask a girl to dance. I slid and bobbed clumsily, maneuvering my way through crowds on the dance floor and those around me looked on in interest and stood a safe distance. I was an unusual sight and some kids might have made cruel jokes, but I was growing more confident. I, the hopeless romantic, still looking for the girl of my dreams. So fragile were my emotions, so needy was my heart, I was thinking, *I've met her.* When she told me that she didn't want to be my girlfriend and she didn't want to "go with" me, I was crushed and blamed it on my injury. Right or wrong, good or bad, I would spend the next years blaming everything on the accident, including that first rejection.

My mom drove me home the night of the dance, and she probably knew something had happened when I came home and slammed the door to my room. She would have heard me cry.

CHAPTER FOURTEEN

BUCKLE UP

"The boy needs to buckle up. What's done is done. He can't go on feeling sorry for himself. He needs to pick himself up by the bootstraps and move on," I heard Hank say as he tossed his cowboy hat onto the kitchen table one night when he got home. "We're not doin' him favors lettin' him bellyache and coddling him every time things don't go his way."

"He's been through a lot," Mom said. "We can't expect him to just forget about what's happ --"

"We damn well can and for his sake we will!" Hank barked, interrupting her. The conversation was the same day after day, night after night, as Hank and my mom watched their son slowly change from a once happy, vibrant boy to an insolent, self-absorbed teen. Every time I talked about trying out for baseball next season or playing football again, I think my mom's heart broke a little more. And my fits—my mood swings—after four months were becoming unbearable. She understood me more than anyone, and understood my frustration. But she couldn't feel my pain, my physical pain. Mom had no idea how my fingers hurt to grip a pencil, or how I strained and fought against the intense aching in my arms—just to comb my hair. But she knew I was not the same boy I used to be.

"He needs to be a man. He's alive for God's sake," Hank would say. "It could've been a lot worse. You'd think he'd be thankful just for that. But he's got his head in the clouds." I don't know if Hank loved me or felt as bad as anyone about the accident and how my world had changed. But he believed the best thing for me was to forget about the past.

My dreams had gone up in smoke. Every time he saw me feel sorry for myself, I think he wanted to shake me. Or wanted to think of me as weak. Hank's philosophy was: That's not how a man behaves. Not a rancher. Not a cowboy. Not his son. Not the boy he was raising. If I brought up my injury, a common answer from Hank would have been, "You're still thinking about that? You need to move on. That's old news." From that point on, I was no longer allowed to talk about my past. As far as Hank was concerned it was over. We didn't need to mention it anymore.

Eventually, Mom worked up the courage to tell Hank that I wanted to leave. "He wants to move to his father in Cleveland," she said. "You're too hard on him, Hank. And now we're losing him." I remember her voice raised to almost a scream. "He always went to his father's for the summer as part of the custody agreement."

"That's no big deal," Hank shouted at her. "What are you getting so excited about?" But Hank likely knew it might be different. This time, maybe Joe wouldn't come back. "Whatever's best for him," Hank said curtly, as if not wanting to betray his own fear that maybe he had pushed me too far. "He can start fresh there. No one will know him as the kid with the broken neck. They won't be feeling sorry for him and treating him with kid gloves. It'll be good for him."

Since the accident, Mom acted like she didn't want to let me out of her sight—like she felt anxiety every time I left the door when I went back to school, all day until I got home. She was protective, worrying about me in Cleveland with my dad, without her.

"Maybe he should see somebody, a professional," she said lightly to Hank as she busied herself in the kitchen, sweeping crumbs from the kitchen counter after dinner. "Someone who knows about these things," she continued wearily.

"He needs a firm hand. He doesn't need to sit on some shrink's couch and pour his heart out," Hank answered. "Starting today, things are gonna change around here. It's for his own good. You gotta be cruel to be kind sometimes, Judi."

Hank would have the last word, as usual. But I knew my mom worried. Was Hank right? Did he know more about what's best for a boy than she did? Maybe her son would be fine. Maybe he needed to be in Cleveland.

I watched my mom pour a cup of coffee in silence. And I heard her cry herself to sleep again that night.

CHAPTER FIFTEEN

BACK TO SCHOOL

Even though it was considered, I wasn't sent to Cleveland to live with my dad. I stayed in school for the ninth-grade in Olathe, Kansas. I attended only half days, spending the other half with my physical therapist Bob for the next six months. I was no longer an athlete. I was the kid who broke his neck and everyone talked to me as if I were a celebrity and they knew me. Although I enjoyed the attention and longed to be popular, I detested the reasons for it. I didn't want to be known for an injury or a deficit. Or for looking like Frankenstein's monster!

Teachers were sympathetic and made adaptations for me, but the schoolwork didn't seem to be sinking in. They assumed it was my injury but, in fact, I was occupied with other things, namely myself. Aside from being in constant nagging pain, I worried about how I looked. I worried about girls not liking me, like the girl named Karen who had told me bluntly at a school dance that she wouldn't "go with" me. I wanted to be popular and desired with no pity. Knowing that football was out of the question, I tried my hand at drama, participating in two school plays. I directed the first and landed the lead in the second play, *If a Man Answers*. Even I was surprised that I got into drama because of how I looked physically, my body being thin and frail. But I began to develop a love of the stage, not surprising since playing sports was like being on stage in front of an admiring audience.

The physical and emotional challenges were naturally difficult. I became fatigued quickly and felt awkward and self-conscious on the stage. But the thrill of working together with others, of being part of *something* and being on stage was just what I needed. I soaked up the applause.

I had worn the Halo brace since it was was drilled into my skull September 13, 1984, and I got it off December 4, the same year. Removing it was pretty simple and relatively pain free. I felt a relief of pressure when Dr. Striebinger unscrewed it, but I tried to move my head to the left and my head started bobbing like a bobble head. He grabbed it and stopped it. He gave me a Philadelphia neck brace and said it would help support my head. I was excited and went into basketball practice the next day to show everybody that I got my Halo off. A got a big roar of applause from the team. Even though I was a player on the eighth-grade team the year before, I couldn't play in ninth-grade, but I was allowed to be part of things. Same school. Same kids. I wore the neck collar for another month or two, then I didn't have to wear anything.

Freedom!

Getting the Halo off felt like freedom. The first thing I wanted to do was take a bath. I hadn't had a shower or had my full body emerged under water since they first put the brace on. Wanting a bath is one of those things you don't miss until you don't have it.

I looked like I was able-bodied, even though I was far from it. I was able to participate in forensics, competitive speech and drama events and acting challenges. I had a natural flair for impromptu scenes. Being in the school's drama group made me believe I had a talent and kept me sufficiently occupied so not playing sports, while constantly on my mind, was not as much of a burden as it would become during the summer months. And the school year was coming to an end, marked by the commencement ceremony.

"We are so proud to give this year's award to a very special student. One who has met many challenges," the principal began. "I can't think of anyone more deserving for this honor than our own Joe Rhea." The entire audience in the gym stood in thunderous applause as my name was announced for *Drama Student of the Year.* I was surprised and proud, but deep down it was just not enough for me. I had carried on my dream. I was already preparing to try out for the high school baseball team.

CHAPTER SIXTEEN
AVERAGE JOE (NOT REALLY)

"If I hadn't broken my neck, I'd be better than you," I screamed in my mind. But not out loud. I didn't dare. Instead, I kept angry thoughts to myself, breathless with irritation as I smashed a tennis racket to the ground. My teammates and tennis coach had seen this before. I guess I seemed a good-enough player to them and they never understood why I pushed myself so hard, why I stomped and yelled when I made an error on the court. They didn't know that playing tennis was of no consequence to me, the boy who believed he was destined to play baseball.

For the previous years, I had pushed myself beyond reason hoping to regain enough strength to try out for the high school baseball team. The dream was still alive, even as I found new outlets for my energy. I lifted weights, sat on a rowing machine and hit baseballs at a carpet that was hanging in the garage. That's what I did over and over again. And everyday, my anger—the very fuel that ignited my drive and passion, the volcanic rage that poured itself into my recovery—grew a little more. No matter how hard I worked, no matter how much exercise I devoted every day through pain and fatigue, no matter the mental drive—the muscles never got any stronger, for my brain could no longer communicate with those muscles.

That summer between junior high and high school, I played baseball, but it was not the same. Fast pitches would slam into my bat, reverberating through tensed fingers. My swings were weak— the ball would never sail fast and long through the air like it once did. My rocket arm now shot BB's. My dream seemed to be disintegrating before my very eyes, but I didn't give up and people were telling me how lucky I was and how God had blessed me. "Thank God you can walk," I heard over and over again. "God was looking out for you that day, Joe." *Again with the God reason,* I'd think to myself. *I have done a lot of work myself.*

All I felt for certain was that if God had been looking out for me, I wouldn't have broken my damned neck. But I did the only thing I knew how—bottled up my rage and took it out on other things, my baseball bats, my tennis rackets. Or I channeled it into the obsessive strengthening routine I created for myself that I hoped would prepare me for high school tryouts.

Then tryouts began.

For three days I gave my all, pushing through pain and sweat. Believing that I had pulled it off, that I had achieved the goal that I'd set for myself. Then on the third day, the coach delivered the news.

"Rhea, come on in," he said. I followed the coach into his office. "We want you to know that we saw how much effort you gave out there and how hard you have worked. But…You're just not strong enough to play at this level, Joe," he explained.

The word NO that my doctor uttered two years prior when I asked if I would play baseball again came flooding back. *This can't be happening!* rushed through my mind.

I was crushed! Heartbroken.

The focus of my ambitions for two years had been all for naught. I went home that night and cried endless tears, wondering what I could possibly do next. *Why me?* I screamed into my pillow. *Why me?* But true to my competitive nature, even as I lay there, a boy sobbing and gasping, my resolve returned when I looked up at the poster of John McEnroe pinned to my bedroom wall. *I'll try out for the tennis team!* I promised myself. As I laid there, wiping tears from my face, I wondered again, *Why was this happening?* Feeling defeated from failure the previous day, I approached the tennis court nervously.

"Coach Treslot! Is it too late for me to try out for the team?" I was hopeful, and Coach gave me a chance. Within 15 minutes, he walked over and asked, "Are you as good as you look?" I said, "I doubt it, but I'll sure give it my all."

I had success with tennis in spite of my weakness and went on to win ten matches in my junior year of high school and even more my senior year. But I worked hard to hide my weaknesses. I held the racket with both hands and the racket still felt like a 40-pound weight in my frail hands. I made mistakes and blamed them all on my injury as I threw rackets across the court, smashing them into the ground, splintering them as I yelled and screamed. It was ugly. Others looked on as if I embarrassed them and I was embarrassed myself. I kept torturing myself with angry thoughts about how I was a better athlete than they, better than everyone before I broke my neck. But people couldn't understand why I was not the same now, why I was not as good as I once was and never would be again. After all, I bore no scars that they could see. I had no wheelchair. I could walk and run, and I could swing a racket. In fact, I looked the same as I always had, just skinnier.

"Maybe you just need more practice, Joe. Lift more weights, buy a pair of strap-on muscles, lol," one of my teammates kindly offered. "Maybe you're just not as good as you think you are," another taunted. *How could they understand? How could they grasp the torment I had lived with over the past years?* All they saw was success—and me turning my nose up at it. The fact was, I had recovered far more strength, motion and ability than doctors and my therapist had thought possible, but I would never totally regain all of my strength, even as I grew into a man. I would never have the balance and agility that had once set me apart from other athletes. I'd never be "Joe Rhea All-Star" again. But I wouldn't believe that at the time. I wouldn't accept it. And this is where the demons stepped in.

Demons.

Yes, I had them. I was a vessel of torment and a paradox. On one hand, my ambition and drive brought me through a remarkable, some say miraculous, recovery. On the other hand, I could not accept my new limitations. Not so long ago, I couldn't even toss a beach ball, and now I could throw a baseball. But not far enough or fast enough. Not like I had before the accident.

My passion was stronger than my pain. Yet, as I struggled to regain lost strength, my passion, the same force that brought me from the brink of death, left me feeling weak and frustrated. While athletic gifts had helped me to beat the odds, they also left me with an All-Star mind trapped within a below average body. Vanity, my self-concept, compelled me relentlessly through hours, days, weeks of agonizing therapy, for my self-concept knew that only being the best on the field, the best on the team and the best on the court was acceptable.

Negative thoughts haunted me every day, every hour. Sometimes, all I thought about was the accident. Other times, I could only think about the physical pain. Some days, I was filled with determination, only to be trampled the next day by anger and fear. My emotions were out of control and my parents, thinking they were doing what was best, acted as if nothing was wrong, as though I was the same kid I used to be, the same as other awkward teens trying to grow up and maneuver their way through adolescence. My parents had hoped (and so did I) that I'd be better if I went to stay with my father in Cleveland. I did and I stayed only long enough to discover that life was even worse there. No one knew I was the kid who broke his neck and there was no one who would believe it if I told them that I had once been a star athlete.

I grew more unstable everyday as emotions and frustrations tangled and wrangled inside me, threatening to blow in a volcanic rage. *Didn't anyone know that the girls wouldn't like me now? Didn't they know I could be fodder for hungry bullies? If someone decided to push me around, I'd be defenseless.* A dark cloud of anxiety hung over me wherever I went. I could never let my guard down, never relax, never stop worrying. *Would anyone like me now that I had no team and was not an All-Star athlete receiving high-fives and pats on the back? Where would I fit in? How could people forget what a great athlete I once was?*

Heart, mind and body were in constant agony. The very same gifts that aided my recovery were now driving me mad.

Maybe all I needed to help drive the demons away was for someone—anyone—to understand and say, "Yes, Joe. I know how much you hurt. I know how sad you are. I know you were a great athlete. I remember."

But nobody did.

CHAPTER SEVENTEEN
SUICIDE: THE UGLY INTRUDER

No one could say I was a failure at sports due to lack of trying. In fact, no one would say I was a failure at all—except for Joe, myself. Others would say it was a miracle I could throw and swing a bat and run. Over time, I could run really well, but never as fast as I could before.

"It's a miracle, Joe. You should be grateful," people reminded me. "Look what God has done for you," I heard repeatedly. But for me, God played no part in it. It was I who suffered through the pain and humiliation and embarrassment. It was I and I alone who worked myself relentlessly each day until my muscles seized and sweat soaked through my clothes.

When I finally made the summer league baseball team after I got cut from the high school team, it was I who sat on the end of the bench. And it was Jimmy Watkins who sat at the other end of that bench, still the All-Star. Jimmy, of all people, knew the old Joe and comprehended it as best as a teen could, as if he knew in his mind, *How sad it is that Joe Rhea can no longer play, no longer be the player he once was—or even a teammate.* So the next two years continued as they had started with me in constant battle, my weakened body in constant pain and I in constant defense of my bruised ego, crushed and heartbroken. And constantly sitting on the bench.

One day, I realized that what I missed as much as starring on the football team was being *part* of the team and the camaraderie. So I volunteered as Team Manager for Olathe South High School. Team Manager was a fancy way to say "water boy."

Coach seemed only too happy to have me as manager/water boy and maybe was even happy to note that I had finally accepted my limitations. Hank and my mom, too, were pleased that their son had finally accepted a new lot in life and would move on from childish dreams and hopes with a measure of humility. Even I felt some contentment. *At first.*

Being a water boy was difficult work. Each practice, I filled all the five-gallon jugs and lugged them to the field, the weight of them stretching the muscles taut from my shoulders, sending shards of pain downward into my wrists. No one could see how the strain felt crippling my slender fingers and how it stressed every muscle and sinew along my arms, neck and back. There were times I had to take a rest or a shortcut, even when my enthusiasm held up. But, like my muscles, the enthusiasm weakened. My smiles disappeared. This was not how I envisioned being a part of the camaraderie.

Soon, players started to complain about me. Joe is slacking off, they told the coach. *He's too weak. He's lazy.* I was even told I looked like I had anorexia. "You need to eat. Put some muscle on those bones," people told me.

The lack of understanding of my injury and condition was growing as the years passed. When I'd come to my own defense, explaining yet again how good I once was before the accident—my taunters laughed at me, dismissed me, saying, "You're only as good as your last game, Joe!" And my last game was in eighth grade.

The glue that held that team together, the bond which is the hallmark of every great team, eluded me. And as I lay in bed at night, awake with the pain that other teenage boys would not know until old age, I replayed the insults in my head. *Lazy. Slacker. Weak.* One day, half-way through the season, Coach joined the chorus of other voices who slashed at my heart and insinuated that I was lazy! For the last time, I left the bench. For the first time, I was a quitter and the smoldering anger inside me flickered that much brighter. That much hotter.

It was those last days of high school that the idea of suicide barged into my mind like an ugly intruder. With little wonder. I was nearly beaten with frustration and pain over the last few years. My dreams, those perfect and precise dominoes that I once laid out in front of me, fell one into another, swiftly and without mercy. I had tried to escape, tried moving to my dad's in Cleveland, tried new endeavors, but the troubles never relented. The bitterness would not abate. The loneliness lingered and grew. Depression held me prisoner. And I could not turn to my family, my mother, my stepfather. To them, the past was a closed book.

The old me was dying, and the death was slow and unpitying. Suicide could be quick and painless and end the torment and misery. But at least high school was over. And the only thing that had kept me alive was holding on to the dream of falling in love one day. *One day, I will meet the girl of my dreams.* I promised myself I would stay alive for that.

CHAPTER EIGHTEEN
AH, MARY JANE

In the Spring of 1988, I met Stacy and fell in love.

Unfortunately, a relationship with me, the volatile teen, proved challenging and as much as Stacy said she could see the sweet and sensitive side of her new boyfriend, she cringed at my anger and outbursts, my hurtful words, my jealousy. Emotionally, I was crippled, and my scars were baring teeth that snapped at those around me. My Identity was not yet fully in tact and even sexually, I was to discover my childhood injury had left its influence. I was not able to perform in that field, as well as I hoped, either. I was 18-years-old and for most young adults, this was a time in life that meant sexual growth and development of sexual identity, experimentation and the development of positive self-identity. But not for me. It was so humiliating and humbling.

This didn't matter to Stacy, she said. I was in college at University of Kansas in Lawrence and she was still in high school and I'd drive back to Olathe to see her. It wasn't far and sometimes she'd come to campus for parties. I don't know why I had decided to watch a girls' high school soccer game one day, but that's how Stacy and I met. I was standing on the sideline and she was playing. After the game, I don't remember what I said to her…it was silliness…but we spoke. I started going to watch her games. She was playing goalie one time when an easy ball went through her legs and scored for the opposition. She was really upset. When the game was over, she was short with me. Nothing to say.

That night, she drove over to my house to say, "I feel bad. I came to apologize to you." That's when it all started.

I remember the night a few weeks after we met, when she told me she loved me for the first time. We were sitting out on a little pond at my house, listening to a song, George Michael's *One More Try*…

So if you love me
Say you love me
But if you don't
Just let me go

She squeezed my hand really tight and I knew I was loved. I needed that. But Stacy was in an emotionally abusive relationship with me, and she was smart enough to know it. "I just can't do it anymore, Joe," she told me after about a year. "It's too hard. Your mood swings just got too hard."

I saw her a lot after that because I was a good friend with her brother. She started dating another guy. It was really hard to see her not being with me. I didn't handle it well at the time. Like every disappointment I faced, I blamed the break up on my injury. I could no longer control my bitterness, even as I knew how self-pitying I sounded. But a need to be understood was stronger than ever—the accident may well have happened yesterday. Emotionally, it *was* like yesterday. I was still that 14-year-old boy who was tossed violently into unexpected waters without a lifeboat and had been treading water ever since, hurled this way and that by monstrous waves and eddies that threatened to pull me under. The more time passed, the more people expected me to put it behind me and the more I clung to it, for it now identified me. It explained my weaknesses, framed my unattainable dreams. My body had healed as much as it ever would, but my mind was crippled, held captive on that football field. But I would soon choose a new way to deal with my hurt.

Around the corner from the campus there was a popular pub for KU students. I tried to drown my sorrows amongst the local revelers. As I shared a beer with a friend one night, I reminisced once again about my accident and how it had changed my life, how it had stolen my dreams, ruined relationships.

"Damn it, Joe!" My friend Robert blurted loudly over the din of voices. "That's all you talk about! I'm sick of hearing it. Shut the hell up, already." Robert immediately said he felt bad for lashing out and wished he could take those words back and I, equally as shocked, headed home to my apartment, hurt and fuming, sinking deeper into depression. *Why can't people understand me?* I cried to myself. *Nobody gives a damn about me! I'll never talk about this again.* But Robert was a trigger. *What he said is important,* I thought. *He needed to jolt me. I have to let go.*

From that night on, I tried to bottle everything up inside. There was no way I was going to have someone speak to me again as Robert had. I held my tongue every time I was about to mention the accident. For a short while, my demeanor seemed calmer, safer, but in truth, the calm exterior was a mere mask for the volcano churning inside with toxic flames that wanted to erupt and engulf me and everyone around me. Except for when I slept. Sleeping was the only release I could find for myself and I slept whenever I could. When I was awake, my tongue was a sword that cut people in two. My broken heart, each shattered piece, was a shard that sliced and scraped against those nearby. There was no release, not a moment of peace so long as I was awake. And thoughts of suicide continued to creep into my mind. Until I discovered *Mary Jane.*

Marijuana was my next love.

As an athlete, I was anti-everything. Smoking, drinking, drugs. But my best friend (and you know who you are!) introduced me to marijuana for the first time. I was sitting in my car with his cousin and I remember thinking, *I'm not angry. I don't feel angry.* Finally, I experienced rare moments of contentment, even bliss. For the next few years, not only was my physical pain eased but my emotional pain was covered like a baby in the safety of a flannel blanket. Weed gave me the escape I needed from my troubles and from myself and my suffering psyche. It seemed to lift my depression and dark thoughts. It kept suicide—that noxious intruder—from entering my mind. And it certainly made me a more pleasant person to be around at times. Between marijuana and sleep, I continued to cope and friends continued to cope with me.

It had been four years since a stormy relationship with Stacy and I felt ready for love again. It was 1992. I was in my early 20s and living in a party house with three other college students when I met Leah. Incredibly, I still held vague hopes of one day playing professional sports and I felt my days at college were aimless and empty. No new goal had replaced the old and I roamed from class to class, course to course, going through the motions of a university student. I was already enamored with marijuana when I met Leah and immediately fell in love with her. She was a beautiful Greek girl with olive skin and sparkling green eyes and a perfect smile framed by a sateen of black tresses. The first time I saw Leah was at a bar and I remember thinking how gorgeous she was. The next summer, I saw her at her apartment pool. We didn't have a pool so we went to everybody else's. "There's that girl," I said to my roommate. He knew her roommate and somehow we all got together that evening. The next night, we got together again and went to *Guitars and Cadillacs,* a country-western bar in Kansas City. I told Leah I thought she was the most beautiful girl at KU. She probably heard that a lot, but as you know, it doesn't matter who says it to you. It's who you want to say it.

We started seeing each other and we were together for a year and a half. Leah came from a good family and I met her parents over a New Year's weekend. I remember on New Year's Eve, she asked me, "Where do you want to be in five years?" I didn't have an answer.

When I think of her now, I think of a girl who looked like she had gone to finishing school. I still have a picture of when we were on a date and she was wearing a red sweater with buttons down the front. She was stylish. She was elegant. We were in love. But Leah was cautious with affairs of the heart and put me through a lengthy dating ritual. For one, she didn't approve of my daily drug use. So I lied. I told her I gave up smoking and worked hard at keeping the truth from her. I lied to my friends, my mother and my father, too. I was still dealing with my issues. I was a toxic mix of pain, lies and drugs. Days were a nauseous ride of highs and lows, laughter and depression, sleeping and waking. I remember her telling me, "I don't understand how one moment you can be so sweet, so endearing, and the next minute have a mouth of poison."

I had held my promise to keep my accident and injury to myself and not explain about the past. She might have been more forgiving of my tirades and outbursts, even my drug use, if she had known what demons I battled. But she didn't like it. One night when we were in her apartment in our last year of college, she said, "I don't see a future for us, Joe."

She knew when she graduated, she'd go back to school in her home town. She was planning her future at age 22. I was just thinking about my next time getting stoned. Like others before her, she broke it off with me that night. She never really spoke to me again. She would never know how I would one day look back and want forgiveness. At any rate, if things had worked out, she would have been *Leah Rhea*. So perhaps it's for the best.

CHAPTER NINETEEN

AROUND AND AROUND

I was bruised and battered and I couldn't tell who I was.

It was 1994 and the world was changing rapidly. Early in the year, Los Angeles was hit by a major earthquake and left over 70 people dead and more than 10,000 injured. The world I saw was in chaos and blood was shed all over. Over the next months, as many as 800,000 people would be slaughtered in Rwanda as a merciless genocide against the ethnic group Tutsi began. And four men were convicted in the shocking World Trade Center bombing. Americans were glued to their TV sets as the O.J. Simpson saga unfolded and the new era of celebrity obsession began. Netscape was just released and there were hardly 18,000 websites on the World Wide Web, the latest of which was then whitehouse.org, a bold initiative by President Clinton. And the world had witnessed the first live web cam, which focused on a coffee pot in a computer lab in England!

Attention was drawn to the tragic and deadly AIDs epidemic and *Philadelphia*, the first movie to deal with that subject hit the big screens. Bruce Springsteen performed the best-selling song from the *Philadelphia* soundtrack and as soon as I heard it, I recognized the aching loneliness and aimlessness in the haunting verses.

I saw my reflection in a window
I didn't know what I felt
I was unrecognizable to myself

The years at college seemed to drag on at first, but finally they were over and in my mid-20s, adult life faced me. I sensed the years had sped by quickly, leaving more emptiness in their wake. And I had no college degree to show for it.

Never straying away from a love of sports, I landed a summer job at the Alvamar golf course in Lawrence and I spent the days going round and round the greens, cutting grass that hardly had a chance to grow. It was a metaphor for my life. Around and around those greens I went in an endless, aimless loop with a walkman attached to my side, playing lonely and desperate songs over and over again. (There wasn't even baseball to cheer me up, for the World Series was cancelled due to a player's strike which lasted 232 days.) And no matter how many miles I put on that ride-on, I could never escape—not from myself. Not from the tangled mess of emotions that held me captive. Not from endless thoughts about Leah and our failed relationship. Not from the sickening heartbreak and fear that I would never know a lasting love. Although I was young and free and worked outside in the summer's heat and that should have been the best time of my life, my depression sank deeper and anger churned always in the pit of my gut.

I walked the avenue till my legs felt like stone
I heard the voices of friends vanished and gone

At night, I'd go home to my apartment and roommates and a house full of friends with smoke and beer and more music. Yet, I still felt painfully alone.

The night has fallen, I'm lyin' awake
I can feel myself fading away

CHAPTER TWENTY

YELLOW BRICK ROAD

Nervously, I walked downtown to a corner office in Kansas City where Judy Moore a Clinical Psychologist, met with "clients." A line from an old movie kept bouncing through my head: *He's off to see the wizard.* I didn't remember the last time I had heard that song, but there it was, bouncing from neuron to neuron, in between my thoughts...*off to see the wizard.*

Although things in my life seemed to remain endlessly the same, times were changing in society and, thanks to public information campaigns, people were becoming more liberal and accepting of the idea of mental illness. It had been ten years since my accident and the stigma of emotional illness was beginning to diminish. I was still living in Lawrence and at my roommate Ken's suggestion—insistence—I finally decided it was time I sought help.

I didn't know how I could I possibly tell this stranger all that I had been through and all that I was feeling. *How could she help?* I wondered. *How will our session begin? Will I look at inkblots and tell all I see are cages and prison cells? Maybe I'll have a psychological test to fill out like I learned in psychology class. I wish I had paid more attention to that.*

He's off to see the wizard...

My step quickened as I kept pace with the song that played in the background of my brain. Maybe Dr. Moore will ask, *What brings you here today and I will confess. I'm a volcanic rage seething, waiting to explode on someone who changes the channel or eats the last of the peanut butter. Or maybe I'll tell her how a storehouse of tears rests behind my eyes, always ready to gush forth.*

My mind raced thinking of all things I wanted to say, wondering if I'd have the courage, wondering if I'd sound silly or, even worse, if I'd sound perfectly normal and she would send me on my way. *Will I have to lie down on a leather sofa? I don't think I can do that. Too personal. Will she use a tape recorder?*

Whatever happens, whatever unfolds, I hoped it would be a new beginning. I hoped my life would change, I would change—starting that day. Immediately. Now.

When I arrived at the office, I was expecting dark and broody mahogany furniture and paneled walls. But I saw potted plants and breezy curtains. A female client was leaving as I walked into the waiting area and I felt like I should turn away, look down at my feet, look anywhere so as not to intrude on her privacy. But I peeked out of the corner of my eyes while pretending to study my shoes and I noticed she had been crying. *I don't want to cry,* I thought to myself. *No way am I crying.* I felt a flash of embarrassment for the woman and wished I had not looked.

He's off to see the wizard….Damned song. Get outta my head.

"Joe? You can come in now," the doctor said as she glided across the pale carpeting with hand extended. "I'm Judy Moore."

She didn't seem threatening. There was no sofa in her office. No mahogany. Just a desk, an African violet plant, a table lamp with a plain white shade, a clock, a wicker waste basket, family pictures on books shelves and rows of books lined up from tallest to shortest. The desk was neat, almost sparse—no clutter, no notes, no files. But tissue, a blue box of tissue. Ready.

"Please, have a seat," she offered and it was okay if I called her Judy. I sat in a pink wing back chair with wide, cushioned arms. There were two of them. I chose the one closest to the door. I liked her voice. It was confident, deliberate. Smooth—like a grade school teacher. But not sweet. Not saccharine. Not like the hospital nurses' voices has been.

"Before we get started, I am obliged to tell you a few things," she said. "Although our conversations are confidential, there are limitations to that." She went on to explain how the law states that if I were to tell her that I was planning on hurting myself or others, she would have to break that confidence. She mentioned something else, but my mind had frozen on those words, and replayed them. *Did this mean I couldn't tell her about the suicidal thoughts I battled?* No. She said "planning" to hurt myself. And I never entertained those thoughts long enough to make a plan. The image of a woman, a child in my arms, love—those images chased away that ugly intruder for my desire for love was stronger than my desire for endless sleep.

"Do you have any questions?" She asked, eyes looking directly into mine, the voice reassuring. I had none.

"*So, how are* you?"

Simple. *How could it be that simple? She's asking how I am,* I thought incredulously. People say that to the checkout girl at 7-Eleven. They say that to strangers on elevators, a quick nod and, "How are ya?" Old friends, say "How ya doing?" and try to sound sincere. But no one was. No one was sincere. That was a filler. No one really wanted to know, no one wanted to be burdened with my hideous, messy truth. Except Judy. Judy Moore *wanted* to know.

Without warning, the storehouse of tears, that tsunami surged up from the deepest parts of me and came swooshing in. My heart hurt. My eyes hurt. I was a dam, threatening to break at any second. I panicked, trying to control the surge. I couldn't talk. If I spoke the dam would break. It would spill out all over the carpet in great gushes. Not enough tissue.

*He's off to see the wizard…*I did the only thing I could. Silently, I sang the song once more in my mind—deliberately—until the wave of sopping pain subsided. Until my throat released that choking ball of agony that was stuck behind my Adam's apple. *What could it mean? How could such a simple question take a grown man to his* *knees?* One minute, I was standing safely and firmly on the shore and the next minute, being swooped away by the wave that had been building for a decade.

...the wonderful wizard of Oz.

Judy was finally a sympathetic ear I could talk to. She was supportive and she understood. She nodded and smiled when I spoke and she made me feel affirmed. She listened. Yes, what had happened to me was tragic. I would never be the All-Star baseball player I once believed I was destined to become. But now what? *What will you become, Joe? Who will you become? How can you be like Frank?*

After only a few sessions, Judy wrote in her notes: "Joe's depression is probably best described as experiencing a dulling of the senses, which in turn helps him with his excessive physical pain. His depression is a particularly painful experience...his dulled senses can worsen his feelings of desperation."

She had me pegged. *But could she help me leave an old dream and find another? I wanted to be like Frank--always. Could I still be like my hero, Frank White, yet not play baseball? Could I find another way to light up the world? Light up a room? When one dream dies, must another take its place.*

What's more, Judy said the words I had so desperately needed to hear.

"It's okay to feel that way. You have a right."

It was okay.

I didn't see the *off to see the wizard* refrain as a metaphor at the time. In reality, maybe it was. I needed a wizard, someone who represented power and wisdom and had the skill to help me with no prescription pills. No medication. In that one second and if for only that one moment when Judy said I had a right to feel the way I felt, the albatross that had been hanging so heavily around my neck was released. It was as if it took flight, if only for a while.

Darkness still hovered, the moods remained a burden—always erratic, always emotional—but the long and slow path to healing had begun. Or so I thought.

CHAPTER TWENTY-ONE

VAIL

The wind and snow whipped around my Volkswagen Jetta, a 1988 model, all-white with black leather interior. It was a stick shift. I loved it. But the snow was like gossamer veils, blinding the driver. Like reckless fingers playing with a toy, the white wind shook the Jetta and swooped under the sturdy frame. In the distance, I could see the fuzzy blur of red taillights. *Just follow the taillights in front of you and you'll be all right, Joe,* I thought. *Unless we go off the road into the two-foot ditch on the icy shoulder, like other drivers did.* Cars were tossed everywhere as Kurt and I made the 700-mile road trip from Kansas to Colorado. Kurt was going to be my roommate when we got to Colorado. It was November 14, 1994, and winter storms had started early that year.

My fingers tightened on the steering wheel. Even after all the years since my injury, there was a feeling that clung to me all the time: the feeling of impending danger…the feeling of unexpected disaster that was stronger, meaner, than my body. This situation called for perseverance. Without the benefit of snow tires, with the small car packed with all our belongings—threatening to become deadly projectiles should we smash into a guardrail or oncoming truck— we kept driving right into a major winter storm past Idaho Springs. It would be 14 hours before we reached our destination and joined Ken, my roommate from KU.

Unlike me, Ken had plans for after graduation. He had heard about jobs at the famous Vail Ski Resort and wasted no time in packing up and going there. When he arrived, he phoned Kurt and me to tell us there were still rooms available and invited us to join him. The idea of a fresh start excited me. I was always looking for a fresh start. I'd been moving from one parent's home to another, one town to another, one school to another—hoping my troubles wouldn't follow me. But they did. Maybe this time would be different.

I had to figure out how to finance the trip. Mowing greens all summer earned me just enough money for a scant bit of food and fun—and drugs. I was an adult then and was expected to make my way in the world. Still, I would have to turn to my parents yet again and ask for money if I wanted to make the trip. I argued with myself over whether to call my mom and Hank, but the idea of the mountains, the fresh crisp air, the excitement...the notion of living life as a *ski bum!* was too irresistible. I made the call.

"I'll need about two thousand dollars to get set up," I said. Sheepishly.

Two thousand dollars was no small sum for any parents and they had held many discussions and arguments about me and bailing me out over the past years and this one went the same as all the others:

"He's 24 years old! He needs to stand on his own two feet," was Hank's position. "He's a man now!"

But they finally agreed to give me the money and Hank even made arrangements for a place to stay until we got settled. I sensed that they knew how desperate I was so they offered the money with mixed feelings. I was used to mixed feelings. I had many feelings from excitement to guilt to fear. It was excitement to be leaving... guilt for taking the money and fear of the unknown. I felt a little anxious that I would once again get hurt on those majestic hills. That sense of being fragile and breakable had never left me. Nevertheless, I set off to Colorado with Kurt and began the next chapter of my life. *Yes*, I thought, *Go to the mountains. Maybe some good will come of it.*

SPILT MILK

Kurt and I moved into our temporary quarters—a majestic timeshare at the foot of the mountain. It was just like out of a storybook with grand oak beams and a massive fireplace that we piled high with wood and set ablaze. A Jacuzzi was built right outside the back door. For me, it was all too romantic and I wished longingly for someone to share it with, someone besides Kurt. I was still and always would be looking for that one great love. But we would have to find our own place soon and even ski bums had to hold down a job. The average rent I was used to was $533 a month, but in Vail it was much higher. Within a week, Kurt and I found a place to live in a house in Eagle-Vail with three other roommates. It was beautiful and spacious, nestled in a valley below with large windows on the south wall, always letting in the sun and warmth. We could see Beaver Creek Resort from the windows. But the price was prohibitive. We would need $900, or $450 a month each to share a bedroom, just for a place to sleep. We needed work.

"Try one of the sporting goods store," Ken suggested, looking very much the ski professional in his stonewashed Levi's tucked into Sorel boots, bright yellow vest and long-sleeved microfibre ski shirt in corn-flower blue. No one wanted to look bulky on the slopes anymore, not since the fashion industry discovered the ski industry. Even Polo and Ralph Lauren had come out with a new line for skiers. It didn't take long for people to transform in a ski town. That was perfect for me. I found a job and began working at Beaver Creek Gear at the resort. I needed to outfit myself and maybe there would be discounts. And the work would not be labor-intensive which would give me the added benefit of a discounted ski-pass. I couldn't wait to hit the slopes and become the best skier in Vail.

One typical Thursday evening, the roommates were busying themselves with plans and phone calls when Kurt got the devastating news that his mother had died. She fought a long battle against cancer and even though the news was expected, it was difficult to accept. He needed to be alone. He needed fresh air.

"Can you pick up some milk while you're out?" I asked. Kurt said nothing and probably couldn't believe I was asking him to run errands. His mother just died, for Christ's sake.

I looked through the local paper to check the movie listings at Crossroads Theatre. *Interview with a Vampire* and *Shawshank Redemption* were still playing. I'd heard great things about those movies, but there was no way I was going to miss skiing. I was getting angrier each day that my skiing was not improving as much as I wanted. I wanted to be the best, naturally. And old and ugly feelings began to resurface. I was becoming increasingly agitated. Anything could set me off.

When Kurt got back, I looked up from the paper and noticed the milk he had placed on the table. It was 2% milk. It was *2%* and not whole. (What you are about to read now I am the most embarrassed I have ever been.) I flew into a mad rage.

"How could you be so fucking stupid? You know I don't drink that shit. Why don't you get your damned head out of your ass!" I screamed at Kurt and tossed the milk carton across the room, splattering its creamy contents against the wall. Kurt was in shock. How could anyone be so self-centered and insensitive? He had had enough. "Who the hell does he think he is?" Kurt had a right to think.

It was the last straw for me. I had finally hit rock bottom.

I went to my room, slammed the door, panting from my rage. Alone in my room, I was embarrassed, humiliated and confused. *How could*

I have done that? What the hell was I thinking? He's my friend and I treat him like that?

Tears streamed down my face. I sobbed from shear humiliation. I was ashamed. *I don't want to be this person anymore. I don't want to be so angry.* Without hesitation, I knew what I needed to do. I picked up the phone and called Judy Moore, the psychologist I had seen before.

"Judy, it's Joe Rhea. I need help, and I need it now," I pleaded. I can't take it anymore. I'm going crazy. I'm losing control and I'm going out of my mind with anger."

"Joe, maybe you should try the drug called Prozac," she said. "Many people find this helps them a lot. It improves their mood, helps them think more clearly so they can…"

"Whatever it takes," I interrupted. "I'll do whatever you say."

I broke into inconsolable crying as Judy waited on the other end of the phone in silence.

CHAPTER TWENTY-THREE

EPIPHANY

After Dr. Moore, Judy, suggested I find a doctor in Vail to prescribe medication, I found one the next morning. The doctor gave me a questionnaire to fill out. Yes, *I sometimes have thoughts about suicide…The joy seems to have gone out of my life…I no longer enjoy the things I used to enjoy…I feel fatigued…I am agitated and move around a lot….*" The questions went on and on and I recognized myself in every one of them. For the first time, I realized just how desperate I was. The doctor realized it, too. He gently prodded me to understand why this young man would be so depressed. Was it simply a problem with brain chemistry or had something precipitated this? I told him my story and the doctor listened intently.

"Why did you wait so long to get help, Joe?" It was as if he felt sorry that I, the young patient in front of him, had suffered needlessly all this time when there were medications on the market that could help me cope, help me be myself and be whole again.

"It's nothing to be ashamed of, Joe. Your brain has a fluid called serotonin which helps to regulate your moods. The serotonin levels can drop off, which causes clinical depression. Sometimes it can be caused by a traumatic event, like yours, for instance. All those feelings you've described—that's depression. And it's an illness…not a weakness."

I needed to hear that. I needed to hear that I was not weak. The doctor wrote out a prescription for Prozac which I filled the same day. I was eager to take the first pill although I worried a little about the effects it would have on me, but the doctor had told me not to expect anything drastic. "It will be two to three weeks before you notice a difference," he'd said. And it's a gradual thing." *Three weeks*, I thought. *Would Kurt stay with me that long? Could he last that long?*

After his mother's funeral, Kurt had returned to Vail and when I asked his forgiveness for my outburst, he was forgiving. I explained how sorry I was and how ashamed. Kurt said he understood. He had a good heart. He forgave me. We lived together for the next ten months in Vail. Then Kurt moved to Oklahoma to live with his girlfriend and I stayed in Colorado.

Four days after I started taking the Prozac, I woke up from a dead sleep at 4:00 in the morning. I was wide awake and felt strange. I felt something I had not felt since I was a kid. It may have been excitement. It may have been contentment. It may have even been the faintest sense of happiness. Kurt was already up getting ready for work, when I shot up in bed and looked at him.

"Man, I feel giddy," I said. "It's the strangest feeling. I think those pills are kicking in. But the doctor said it would be weeks."

I was feeling good. And as the weeks passed, I was feeling better everyday. But it was not an artificial feeling. Sometimes my friends would joke about my "happy pills," but pills cannot make one happy. They only made certain adjustments in my brain so I could see and appreciate the true beauty around me, the true goodness of my friends, the goodness of my life. There was nothing artificial about it. I still had bad days and bad moods like anyone else, but anyone would envy me now—living my dream, playing sports, skiing, working part-time, meeting new people and living with my friends in the most exciting place to be in winter. The darkness that usually hovered over me was slowly starting to lift. Here and there, I could see a faint light—sometimes in a joke, a phone call, a sunny morning. I had been blind to goodness for so long and then, here and there, faint rays of goodness shone through. *Life could be good. Maybe.*

Then one day it hit me just how lucky I was.

One early March morning, my friends and I stood atop the Eagles Nest, top of Vail Mountain and breathed in the crisp Colorado mountain air. Just as we were preparing to descend, a skier flew by and caught everyone's attention. He was laughing out loud with abandon as he sped past our trio. But that's not what caught our attention. The man was skiing in a chair. It was a small seat fastened onto one ski directly underneath him. Under both arms he had two small skis that acted like rudders, extending from his arms and reaching down to the ground.

He was paralyzed from the waist down.

"He looks like he is having the time of his life," Kurt said. Yes, he was. He was Paralyzed and Having the Time of His Life. That realization struck me like I had just discovered gold in his backyard! *And I am having the time of my life!* I thought. Without a word, I pushed off and sped after the skier. I didn't know what I was going to say but I knew I had to talk to him. At the bottom of the mountain, I saw him and we got on the lift. It was a 14-minute ride and it was prophetic. I sat next to him and started off with small chat—beautiful day on the hills…snow is just right…not too powdery. Then I asked him. How did he end up paralyzed.

He explained to me that he had been in a car crash and woke up sometime afterwards to be told he was paralyzed from the waist down. I told him my own story. I told him how I, too, woke one day to be told I was paralyzed. But the stories had different endings. Whereas I spent years in a dark and angry depression, grasping at impossible dreams, this man was open to all that was possible.

"Look around you," the man implored. "See the wonderful beauty that is surrounding you." I looked around and politely nodded. Yep, it was beautiful. I already knew that. Then he said something I'll never forget. "You have to focus on what you can do and not what you can't do.

"Joe, stop right there. What is *really* upsetting you?" The man asked. It was as if he peered into my soul. I felt exposed, naked and vulnerable. I looked again at the world around me. I listened to the silence and would swear I could hear delicate layers of ice melting. Looking toward the snowy south toward Holy Cross, I felt the hair on my neck stand on end. It was breathtaking. An endless expanse of snow-covered mountains, valleys and peaks as far as the eye could see. I was in Vail. The Mountain. And I, high upon it, far away from my worries. Far away from my anger and fear.

I looked toward the east, just slightly, and was intoxicated by the sharp and certain sound of crisp snow crunching. I had not noticed that sound before. I had not been overwhelmed with the beauty until then. Years ago, I was wounded by an accident, then wounded by the world, by people's simple grasp of my complexity, by meaningless words like "Thanks be to God," uttered to make noise and fill silence, uttered by those knowing things could always be worse and who bowed in terror and thanked their God who prevented it from being so. And then, for a brief moment in the silence of those snowy, breathtaking peaks, I wondered if perhaps they were right.

I had gone through enough hardships and challenges in my life. I had focused on all the negatives and it tore me down. In 14-minutes with a man, a paralyzed skier on the lift, I realized I was a walking quadriplegic. I was not somebody in a wheelchair.

As the magnificence of the morning sun spread itself across the glistening ranges before me, I took a deep breath, filling my lungs with mountain coolness and remembering digging my ski poles into the snow, forgetting for a moment the man who had been beside me. The sun exploded through the darkness in my mind like a blinding light. It was as if a million thoughts ran through my mind at once and yet there was total peace and understanding. I felt everything, everywhere, at once. And total serenity. And total joy. I had an epiphany.

CHAPTER TWENTY-FOUR

MOLLY

In August 2008, I finally saw the light. I looked into the eyes of my baby girl and I knew I was finally going to be happy.

I cut the cord in the delivery room, they wrapped her up in a pink and white blanket, laid her in a bassinet and her little head actually turned and looked at me. Seeing my beautiful daughter for the first time—and the second and third and every time thereafter—I knew all my troubles were secondary. I felt my greatest joy. She was my daughter. I was her dad.

Her mother Jenny and I named her Molly Jayne Rhea and carried her home to grow up in metropolitan Kansas City which was home to me. After my adventure in Vail, Colorado, and a short meaningless time in Tahoe, Nevada, I came back to Kansas City. It's the City of Fountains (most in the world, with the exception of Rome) and miles of scenic boulevards and parkways, some overlook the Missouri River from high on the bluffs. Little known is the fact that there are two Kansas Cities divided by State Line Road, a two-lane street with Kansas City, Kansas, on the west and Kansas City, Missouri, on the east. The rivalry in college sports between University of Missouri Tigers and University of Kansas Jayhawks was heated for so long. Believe it or not, the bad blood goes back to the Civil War when Quantrill's Raiders rode in and burned most of Lawrence, Kansas, and killed as many as 190 men and boys. That was 1863 and KU and MU have been playing football against each other since 1891.

Personally, what do I think? What do you think I think? I went to college at KU in Lawrence. I'm a loyal Jayhawk. I have a Jayhawk tattoo. The funny thing is—I swear this is true—Molly has a birthmark that looks a little like a Jayhawk.

Other than the KU/MU rivalry, sports fans are united behind Kansas City Royals—World Series Champions (2015) and Kansas City Chiefs—Super Bowl Champions (2020). Long before, this was home base for the Monarchs, the Negro League teams when Satchel Paige, Jackie Robinson, Ernie Banks and Buck O'Neil played some of their best baseball before Robinson broke the color barrier in 1947. The Negro League Museum is a hot tourist attraction in KC's Jazz District. Besides Monarchs, great Royals major league players of the past are Hall of Fame George Brett and perennial All-Stars like Hal McRae, Paul Splittorff, three-time All-Star pitcher Dan Quisenberry and, of course, five-time All-Star and eight-time Golden Glove Award winner, Frank White. Fans affectionally nicknamed him *Smooth.*

Tailgating at Kauffman Stadium (MLB) or Arrowhead Stadium (NFL), is easy. You can pick up platters of smoky, tangy beef and pork from famous restaurants and BBQ joints, like Gates, Kansas City Joe's, Smokehouse, Jack Stack and the renown Arthur Bryant's— *"Where Those Who Know Real BBQ go!"*

No matter what, Kansas City is a sports town. No matter what, Molly, a pre-teen now, doesn't talk much about sports or watch sports with me. But there was one time we played football together—on TV. KSHB Action News filmed a segment to mark the 18th anniversary of my injury. We went back to the actual spot, Indian Trail football field. They tagged it *Local man uses story to inspire athletes and others* under a banner headline: *From Paralysis to Parenthood.* Like that is a big deal. And it is. Molly and I tossed a ball back and forth for touch football on camera.

She said, "That was really cool."

Molly's not into sports like I am, but she's like me in another way: She doesn't mind being the center of attention. She's very much into theatre and has been in three local movies and lots of stage productions. Can I claim she got that from me? Absolutely! I was a theatre geek for awhile in junior high and high school. I had thought a daughter of mine would love sports as much as I do, but Molly found something else she loves. She's a great little actress and I'm proud of her and equally happy as she is. Some of our favorite moments were when we watched *Glee* together on TV. We'd laugh and sing, sitting on the sofa in a typical living room setting—a big 50-inch Samsung Ultra 4-K High Def television propped up on a stand…photos of Molly and me on the wall…shelves with books I've read over the last 25 years, like *Think and Grow Rich* and the *Harry Potter* series. Molly read a couple of Harry Potters and I used to read a chapter to her every night when she went to bed. I try to make a home that's comfortable.

We liked so many songs in *Glee* and a favorite was Lea Michele singing Katy Perry's *Firework—Baby, you're a firework…Come on, let your colors burst…*We sang along with Lea Michele and we'd talk about the characters and the actors.

"I'd like to be like that," Molly would say.

"The reason you love acting and singing is because you take after your dad," I'd tell her.

She'd go, "Do you think I have what it takes?"

"Of course, you do. There are others out there. If you put in the work and do what others don't do," I'd say, thinking of my role model Frank White's advice. "Do what others don't do. If you do that, then I think you have what it takes."

Then a big smile would come on her face.

Molly and I communicate. We talk. I listen to her and she listens to me. I tell her the most important thing to do is take her education seriously, but I never criticize. I question. What's her motive? Why does she want to do what she's doing? I can't recall a time when I hurt my daughter's feelings and I'm not ever gonna yell at her. That's what

Hank, my stepfather, did to me. I will not be like him as a parent at all. Hank was very short—like it's his way or the highway. Hank was a provider, but if he was loving, he didn't show it. He parented with fear. I was afraid of him. He left a hollow space. When I first started to write this book, I remember Hank said, "Why would anyone want to read a book about you?" He just didn't give a shit.

As I get older, some things about him stand out in my mind, like one of the times he knocked the hell out of me. I was in eighth grade and the drama students were going to Waldo Astoria Theater. It was a school field trip, a big deal, and I cared about how I looked. I got dressed up…I put a dollop of mousse in my hair like everyone did in the 80s. Mousse was something like whipped cream and its wetness shined in my hair (naturally curly hair!). I was ready to go and I was sitting at the breakfast table when Hank took that away.

He came in the kitchen and messed up my hair. I got mad and jumped up from the table. "I didn't realize you were such a baby," he said. And I said, "I didn't know you were such a jerk!"

He struck me and picked me up and threw me against the refrigerator. Mom interrupted and I think that contributed to her plan to leave him. I'm smart enough to know a good father is a father who encourages. You don't have to yell at your children and spank or slap them across the face like Hank did.

You need to be there for your kids.

My dad was not physically present, mainly because of the miles and five states between us. Sure, I went to see him in Cleveland every summer and maybe Christmas, but it felt like he wasn't really there… like he was absent. I don't necessarily hold it against him. I think it was fate. Honestly, I don't think it was right for my mom to leave him and take his young children away one Father's Day with nothing more than a note that said she was sorry. My dad and I are alike as far as being affectionate. I always knew he loved me. He'd say so. When we'd hug and say goodbye, he'd say I love you. Now he'll say it in a text. And now we see each other once a year and talk on the phone every few weeks. But I wish we had been closer.

At Grandma and Grandpa's house, I was treated like a prince. We'd have bacon and eggs for breakfast, coffee with lots of cream and sugar. It's still the way I drink my coffee today. PB&J sandwiches and chocolate milk for lunch. As each day with them turned to dusk, Grandpa lit the coals to a backyard barbecue and we'd sit outside together under the Kansas stars, listening to Royals baseball games on the radio, Grandpa drinking a beer and I drinking Grandma's sweet sun tea made fresh each afternoon. Grandpa was a veteran of World War II, but he didn't talk about it. We talked about baseball and he's the reason I loved the Kansas City Royals as much as I do. And as is typical of the Kansas landscape, a huge field spread out behind the enclosure where no doubt, many pioneers had crossed on their way west. Just beyond, there was a rolling field of grass and a patch of thick woods and an old, abandoned barn. The barn looked ancient and set my imagination wild with ideas of hauntings and curses. I never dared to venture into it, despite my thinking I was a brave kid.

I remember their patio overlooked the sprawl of an immaculate fenced-in yard. It was beautifully manicured and weeded daily by Grandma and Grandpa together. I loved that about those two. They set the stage for my idealistic marriage. They cooked together. They washed the dishes together. She would wash and he would dry. The way they were is what I thought a marriage should be. Molly's mother and my marriage ended after seven years, but Molly's a bright kid and I don't think she feels a lack of affection. Her mother remarried and Molly gets plenty of love from her extended family, her grandparents and me.

Molly was born when I was 38. I had matured. I had worked through years of agonizing physical therapy, but I suppressed my emotional demons until they were too much for me. After years of pain and anger and depression, my spirit was broken and I was desperate. It takes courage to ask for help, but I finally did. Dr. Judy Moore gave me counseling. A doctor in Vail gave me Prozac. Their help gave me clarity, a form of freedom. Professional treatment eased my mind and I could experience *Aha!* moments. Riding in a lift with the paralyzed man who I saw ski down a mountain in Vail was one of them. He opened my mind and in 14 minutes, his words ultimately helped me embrace a life that is worth living.

And I do.

Another *Aha!* came from a chance encounter with a man I met in an Italian Restaurant (where I was working). He happened to be Bernard Franklin, Ph.D, Vice President for Student Life at Mount St. Mary's University in Maryland. We talked and I felt he was wise. He said to me, "You have quite a story. You need to have a career as a motivational speaker."

And I do.

Now I understand. Now I get it. A dark spirit is never going to be good for you, me or anyone. We can change ourselves when we don't want to be angry and bitter anymore. Until I asked for and accepted help for my emotional pain, I was unable to see all that I had to be thankful for. I am a quadriplegic, but I am not in a wheelchair. To rebuild my strength, I worked hard and pushed through pain you can't imagine. Now I walk, I can dance, run, play golf and tennis and I can ski. Change is a long process. You put in the time. The first step is ask for help. Face your torment. Then a defining moment—a transformational change in your life— can happen in minutes. Or in a 14-minute ride in a lift. Or in an unexpected meeting with a gentleman in an Italian restaurant.

I haven't exorcized my demons forever. I live with chronic pain in my body and quadriparesis, weakness in all four limbs. I always will. I still have dark moments, but I acknowledge those feelings and I've learned how to cope.

Long before Molly was born, I had given up marijuana. It no longer served its purpose. I realized it wasn't what I needed to escape the reality of my world. Before that, I had probably been high for a decade, from the moment I woke up to the moment I went to bed. I'm not proud of it.

The truth is, I am a very emotional man. I've cried a lot in my life. But deep down, I always knew in the long run, this moment would happen:

My daughter was born.

I am happy.

Joe Rhea Speaks
Innovative presentations since 2004

Motivational. Educational. Inspirational
Keynote Speaker & Change Agent
Regional. National. International

Just An Average Joe (Not Really)

Thousands of people in the U.S. and abroad applaud the authenticity of real-life experiences Joe Rhea presents in a sports motif. His inspiring story combines years of agonizing recovery from a paralyzing football injury at the age of fourteen, mixed with the ideals of perseverance, optimism and hope. He speaks purposely to everyone who faces (or will face) unexpected trauma, loss and troubling times in personal life and work life.

His voice is warm, wise and vibrant. That's a promise.

Who's Listening?

A top-tier speaker, Joe Rhea captivates a widening audience of all ages: Students, educators, parents, athletes, coaches, veterans and mental health professionals to businesses and corporations, employees, teams, managers and executives.

And he'd like to include you.

——————Joe Rhea Speaks——————

Ask Questions. Choose a Date. Request a Quote
You can find him here:
JoeRhea@JoeRhea.com

Author of
When Life Knocks the Hell Out of You: Beat the Odds

"A dark spirit is never going to be good for you, me or anyone.

We can change ourselves when we don't want to be angry or bitter anymore."

—-*Joe Rhea*

Thanks For What They Say

"Our staff and team were touched by your story and by your inspirational message. Your story is a shining example that serves as a reminder to all of us to welcome every day with the belief and desire to make a difference, and to focus our efforts on being the best that we can be."
Bill Self, Head Coach / KU Men's Basketball

"Thanks for your OUTSTANDING presentation. Last night may well have been the best annual meeting that Tri-County has had! We brought you back for a second time because you have a very compelling story, and you couldn't do it justice in the 20 minutes that you were allotted last year."
Tom Cranshaw, CEO, Tri-County Mental Health

"The story you told of Frank White made me yearn for a day when I can brighten a kid's life, if only a fraction as much as Frank was able to with you. Neither of my goals have been reached yet, so today, when you were delivering your message, I experienced my second goal vicariously through you."
Chris Hayes, Kansas City Royals

"After meeting Joe Rhea, we knew his message and ability to connect with young people was too valuable to keep just to our football players. Rather, we chose to have him present his amazing story of overcoming physical and psychological strategies to our entire student body. His ability to captivate an auditorium full of 14-18 year olds, while not surprising to me, was awesome to witness. In today's short attention span world, his ability to hold his audience captive to every story and life lesson that came from his message is wonderful."
Sam Knopik, Head Football Coach / Pembroke Hill

"As Joe began telling his story and the stories of others he has come into contact with, our student athletes were completely captivated. I have never seen such a quiet yet intrigued group of 300 plus student athletes. As the chair of our drug and alcohol education in the athletic department, I arrange for speakers on a regular basis. I can honestly say that Joe has been one of the most powerful speakers I have seen."
Murphy Grant,
Assistant Athletic Director / KU

**Thoughts from
Bernard Franklin Ph.D, Vice President/Student Life
Mount St. Mary's University**

Life!

In our world of plastic fragility, access to other's fame and wealth, and a microwaved culture of wanting it now, it is easy to throw in the towel. It is easy to measure ourselves by what others have and what we don't. We give up. We quit.

Much of my life's work as a therapist and counselor has been dedicated to supporting men. Men do not often reveal their heart in transparent ways. Men don't openly talk about their tears and their pain. That is true of women, children and young adults, too, although in my experience, it is prevalent among men.

Now here in a book is Joe Rhea's brilliant story of triumph and joy. His narrative exposes a man who has come to see that his life is not measured by how his body moves or does not move, but how he responds to that movement. What makes his personal journey so compelling is that it is told from the vulnerable place of a man's heart.

When I first met him, he was neither an author nor a public speaker. He was then serving at a restaurant. Parts of his body were still paralyzed from his debilitating injury and he had difficulties carrying heavy trays. I was struck, not by his challenges, but his attitude. *You see, it's all in attitude.* It's in how we view our life's circumstances. I knew nothing about this man, but what I sensed exuded from him was a desire to triumph, to win, not to be disgraced, but to overcome! Each time I went to the restaurant was the same. We began to be friends and I discovered that this was not an act. This was Joe. This was authentic Joe.

Now he has come to a place where he has mastered what life has thrown his way. He has arrived. His is a story of a man who has come in sweet surrender to what it is to be totally human in a world obsessed with perfection. Joe is my personal human hero.

Coming out of the world-pandemic of the year 2020, we all need to be reminded that we too can transcend our current condition and become sane with what we have—*life!*

BOOK TALK
for
Book Clubs
& Readers Everywhere

CHAPTER ONE - LIKE FRANK

1) Who was your favorite character? Why was he/she your favorite?

2) What did the character say or do that made you care?

3) In your own words, describe another character

4) What was Joe's worry? Do you think 8-year-old children have worries?

5) Why was Frank White kind to Joe? Why did he agree to visit Joe?

6) Do you remember someone special who was kind to you when you were a child? Who and why was that person memorable?

7) What was Frank White's advice? Was it wise for children and adults?

8) Why did the baseball stories in this chapter matter?

9) If you talked to the author, what question would you want to ask?

10) Did you wonder what will happen in the next chapter? Why?

CHAPTER TWO - LIKE ANY OTHER DAY

1) What was normal about the day?

2) Did a day like Joe described feel familiar to you?

3) How soon did you realize the day wouldn't be normal?

4) Did you suspect danger early in the chapter?

5) What did Joe care about most that day?

6) Was he studious or vain?

7) Why was he in a hurry to leave for school?

8) What did you like or dislike in this chapter?

9) What would you want to ask the author?

10) Did the ending make you wonder what will happen next?

CHAPTER THREE - MVP

1) What was the purpose of this chapter?

2) Was Sanchez an important character? Why or why not?

3) Did the description of the football game seem realistic?

4) Did the description make you feel like you were watching the game?

5) Did you care which team won or lost? Why or why not?

6) What did you like or dislike about this chapter?

7) Why didn't Joe want Hank to know he missed football practice?

8) What would you want to ask the author?

9) Did the chapter end make you wonder what happens next?

CHAPTER FOUR - THE LAST PRACTICE

1) Why does Joe tell a lie to his stepfather, Hank?

2) In your own words, describe Hank's character.

3) Describe the relationship between Joe and his stepfather.

4) Was Hank's expectation reasonable? Was it reasonable for Joe to lie?

5) What did Hank say or do that revealed his character?

6) Was Joe a braggart in the locker room?

7) Did you care if Indian Trail won or lost?

8) When did you realize there was danger ahead?

9) Was there something you'd want to ask the author? Or say to Joe?

10) At the end of the chapter, did you want to know happens next?

CHAPTER FIVE - I'M SORRY

1) Why does Joe apologize after his injury?

2) Is it unusual for children to feel that trauma is their fault?

3) Have you ever blamed yourself for a personal or family trauma?

4) Was there a hero in this chapter?

5) Did you realize the seriousness of Joe's injury? Did you think he'll recover?

6) What emotions did you feel by reading this chapter?

7) What did you like or dislike about this chapter?

8) What would you want to ask the author? Or say to Joe?

9) Did the end make you anxious to know what happens next?

CHAPTER SIX - THE HOSPITALS

1) Who are sympathetic characters? Joe's mom or dad? Hank? The doctor?

2) Did the history of Joe's mother make you understand her and care?

3) Was Joe's father a strong, likable character? Why or why not?

4) Did descriptions of hospital scenes feel realistic?

5) Which scenes made you feel you were there with Joe?

6) What emotions did Joe reveal?

7) What emotions did you feel?

8) Was it strange that Joe imagined himself in war scenes?

9) What did you like or dislike in this chapter?

10) Could you imagine what would happen next?

CHAPTER SEVEN - A SONG FOR MOM

1) What did the author mean when he used the word plaintively?

2) What was the overall tone or mood to this chapter?

3) How did it make you feel?

4) How did you feel about Joe's mother?

5) As a mom, son or daughter, did you relate to Joe's mother?

6) Did the song lyrics enhance or distract the story line?

7) Did you like or dislike this chapter? Why or why not?

8) Was there a hopeful note somewhere in the narrative?

9) Did the chapter end make you want to know more?

CHAPTER EIGHT - ALONE

1)   What was the saddest or most poignant line?

2)   Have you or someone you know experienced such loneliness?

3)   Describe where, why and when?

4)   Was Joe's pain and emotional pain only about himself?

5)   Did you like or dislike this chapter? Why or why not?

6)   At the end, did you foresee a hopeful story? Why?

CHAPTER NINE - HALO

1) Why dId Joe think first about his football team when he woke up?

2) Did he worry about his mother? How do you know?

3) Was the doctor's explanation of Joe's condition clear? Was there hope?

4) What did Joe foreshadow? Did it make you curious about his future?

5) Who were your favorite or least favorite characters? Why?

6) Did you see, feel and hear the process of the Halo being installed?

7) What of that experience was most vivid or wincing?

8) What was the worst sound?

9) Why again did Joe imagine a war scene?

10) Did the end paragraphs signal hope or concern?

CHAPTER TEN -
SCREWS IN YOUR BRAINS

1) Did Joe's reaction to therapy show confidence, defiance or denial?

2) What did he think or say that showed his attitude?

3) Why did one physical exercise make him feel "silly?"

4) What theme in another imagined war story felt rational in Joe's mind?

5) Did prayer feel rational and helpful to him?

6) Why did the Rocky Balboa movie feel helpful to him?

7) What lesson did Joe learn from a child with a physical disability?

8) Was there a lesson for you, the reader?

9) Did you like or dislike this chapter? Why?

10) What did you think (or hope) might happen next?

CHAPTER ELEVEN -
WHERE IT ALL BEGAN

1) When and why did Joe say, "This was my moment!"

2) When and why did Joe say, "...the sweetest words I had ever heard."

3) What was the general tone or mood of this chapter?

4) What lifelong decision did Joe make as an 8-year-old child?

5) What were his ardent dreams?

6) Joe said, "I'd like to think I was the object of _____"

7) Why was Jimbo Watkins an influential character?

8) Who were your favorite characters? Why?

9) What did Joe do that "couldn't be done?"

10) Did you like or dislike this chapter? Why?

CHAPTER TWELVE - FIRE WITHIN

1)   What did nurses call a miracle?

2)   How did Joe react to his progress being called a miracle?

3)   Did physical therapist Bob push too hard?

4)   What fueled Joe's anger—the fire within?

5)   What would you want to ask or say to Joe?

6)   Did you like or dislike this chapter? Why?

7)   Did you wonder what will happen next?

CHAPTER THIRTEEN - KID IN THE CAGE

1) Did you sympathize with Joe, a teenager who felt trapped?

2) Did you sympathize with Joe's mother or his stepfather?

3) Did Joe seem more concerned about himself or about his mother?

4) How well did he handle going back to school?

5) Since he could use one arm, did you think he'll completely recover?

6) Given his physical condition, what was Joe worried about?

7) What was your reaction when Joe "got up the nerve" to go to the school dance?

8) What was your reaction to the girl he asked to dance?

9) Did you understand why Joe cried?

10) At the end of the chapter, did you wonder what would happen next?

CHAPTER FOURTEEN - BUCKLE UP

1) What was your opinion of Hank?

2) Did you agree with Hank's advice about how to handle his stepson?

3) Did you feel worried about the "once happy" Joe?

4) Did you feel sympathy for his mother?

5) Did you agree Joe should stop thinking about his injury and move on?

6) Did you agree Joe should "see a professional?"

7) If you were Joe's parent, sister or brother, or friend, how do you think you would feel?

8) Did you think Joe should go live with his father in Cleveland?

9) At the end of this chapter, did you wonder what will happen next?

CHAPTER FIFTEEN- BACK TO SCHOOL

1) Read the 2nd paragraph again, then answer question 2

2) Do you understand and relate to the thoughts—the good and the bad—running through Joe's mind?

3) Were you surprised Joe "got into drama" despite his physical condition?

4) Did what happened in the last paragraph surprise you?

5) Why was Joe's reaction mixed?

6) At the end of the chapter, did you wonder *What Now?*

CHAPTER SIXTEEN -
AVERAGE JOE (NOT REALLY)

1) What was your reaction to Joe's character in this chapter?

2) Did you understand his frustration?

3) Is he a sympathetic character, even more now than before?

4) Are you surprised that he still has pain from his injury?

5) How would you react in his circumstances? Would you give up?

6) Have you been in a situation where you said, "Why me? Why did this happen to me?"

7) Why was a poster of John McEnroe an inspiration?

8) What was your reaction to teammates who taunted him?

9) Did you understand why Joe said he grew more unstable every day?

10) At the end of the chapter, do you think there's hope for his recovery?

CHAPTER SEVENTEEN - SUICIDE

1)   What is your reaction to this chapter?

2)   What would you say to Joe?

3)   Did you feel like giving up on him?

4)   Did you feel there was a sign of hope?

5)   At the end of the chapter, did you wonder what happens next?

CHAPTER EIGHTEEN - AH, MARY JANE

1) Did this chapter feel more hopeful than those of the past?

2) Who are the dominant characters? Are there two or three?

3) What is your reaction to Stacy?

4) What is your reaction to Leah?

5) Did you like one more than the other?

6) Did you feel each one made the right decision about Joe?

7) What was your reaction to Joe's change in behavior?

8) What emotion did Joe reflect at the end of the chapter?

9) Did you wonder what he'll do next?

CHAPTER NINETEEN - AROUND & AROUND

1) What was the purpose of the second and third paragraphs?

2) In what way did the brief cultural history define Joe's character?

3) Did you feel the author's use of lyrics enhanced the story? Why?

4) Does the title *Around & Around* fit the chapter?

5) What was Joe's "sickening heartbreak and fear?"

6) Have you, like Joe, ever felt "painfully alone?"

7) At the end of the chapter, are you ready to give up on him?

8) At the end of the chapter, do you wonder what will happen?

CHAPTER TWENTY -
YELLOW BRICK ROAD

1) What was the purpose of a refrain from the *Wizard of Oz*?

2) What issue had changed in public information campaigns?

3) Did the catchy *Yellow Brick Road* refrain stick in your head, too?

4) Why did Joe decide to see a psychologist?

5) Did you feel it took courage for him to reveal his deep feelings?

6) He hoped it would be a new beginning? Was it?

7) What did the psychologist say that Joe "desperately needed to hear?"

8) In what way was *Off to See the Wizard* a metaphor?

9) Would Joe finally find happiness and peace of mind?

10) Did you wonder what will happen next?

CHAPTER TWENTY ONE - VAIL

1) What did you expect since this chapter was near the end of the book?

2) Will Joe suffer the rest of his life? Is there hope?

3) Was he still a conflicted character? A strong character or a sympathetic character?

4) Were you surprised he could ski, even though he was a quadriplegic?

5) Why did you think his stepfather agreed to finance Joe's trip to Vail?

6) Have you ever gone skiing..and how much fun was it?

7) At the end of the chapter when Joe said "maybe something good will come of it," did you believe something would?

CHAPTER TWENTY TWO - SPILT MILK

1) Did Joe's behavior make you feel angry with him?

2) Were you ready to give up on him?

3) Why was Joe still so angry ?

4) What is your opinion of Kurt?

5) If you were Kurt, would you leave and not come back?

6) What would you have said to Joe if you were Kurt?

7) Did you care enough about Joe to wonder will happen next?

8) Was there a sign of hope?

CHAPTER TWENTY THREE - EPIPHANY

1) Why did Joe wait so long to get professional help?

2) What did the doctor in Vail say that Joe needed to hear?

3) What did the doctor do that Joe needed?

4) What was your opinion of Kurt in this chapter?

5) What was your opinion of Joe?

6) Why did Joe say other people would envy him?

7) What advice did the paralyzed man give to Joe?

8) Did you agree with the man's advice?

9) What emotion did you feel when you began to see Joe's transformation?

10) After following Joe's rigorous and often hopeless journey, did you wonder what will happen in the final chapter? Did you care?

CHAPTER TWENTY FOUR - MOLLY

1) Describe what you learned and how you felt when you read this chapter?

2) Consider scenes, descriptions, characters, sports stories, setting and landscape and setting and more.

3) Out of 24 chapters, did you have a favorite?

Order from the Author
and Save!

signed copies
When Life Knocks the Hell Out of You
Beat the Odds

by
Joe Rhea

Order online
JoeRhea@JoeRhea.com
Rheatalkingsports@gmail.com

$2.00 off cover price - Limited Time Offer
(not currently available on Amazon)

When Life Knocks the Hell Out of You: Beat the Odds

From the Editor:

If you've visited the photo gallery and read through chapters and testimonials, you have an understanding of what a stand-up guy the author is. And I do mean stand up.

Through unstoppable drive and endless pain Joe Rhea was determined to never be confined to a wheelchair. He now stands as a mobile and active man of achievements. He also stands for social issues and served first as an advocate of the *Think First: National Injury Prevention Foundation's* mission. The purpose is to educate and prevent brain, spinal cord and other traumatic injuries and disabilities, often caused by vehicle crashes, violence, falls, sports and unsafe driving practices.

What I like to say about Joe Rhea is—I knew him when.

When the manuscript for *When Life Knocks the Hell Out of You* had laid dormant and unfinished for more than a decade.

When the manuscript was taken out and dusted off and polished and sent to a publisher.

When he was excited and a nervous wreck all at the same time, waiting to cross the finish line as a published author.

A question his stepfather asked him—*Who'd want to read a book about you?*—kept popping up in Joe's mind. And Joe wondered, *Who would?*

So, Readers! You've answered the question. You've read it. For sure, authors appreciate their readers and are glad to get a response. Here's another question:

Should Joe Rhea write a sequel and continue the narrative of his life story? What would you want to know?

JoeRhea@JoeReha.com   rheatalkingsports@gmail.com

My Hero...Frank White's arm around me, age 8, at my Cub Scout meeting. He made every kid feel like a million dollars when he gave them his autograph. That's when I knew I wanted to be like Frank White.

Two Trophies. Proud Kid...A trophy in each hand. One for winning All-Star baseball tourney and one for me, MVP. I tried to look like a tough guy, but I felt so proud.

Soldier Dad...Joe Rhea Sr., Staff Sergeant, 101st Airborne U.S. Army. In uniform in Vietnam. Look at his powerful arms. Mine would have been similar instead of being sticks after my injury. Dad lived in Cleveland. I lived in Kansas City, but I always knew he loved me.

My Mom...One of my favorite pictures of Mom, Judi, with her bright eyes and pretty face.

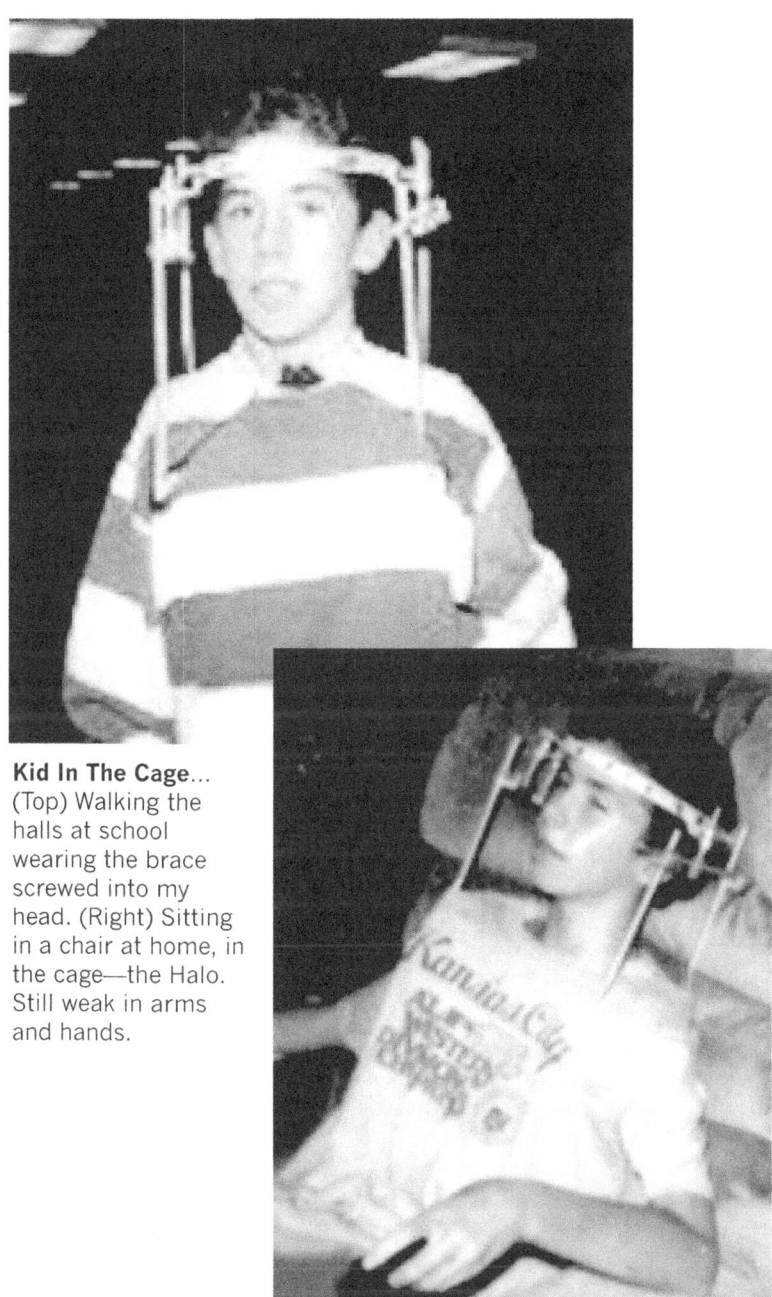

Kid In The Cage...
(Top) Walking the halls at school wearing the brace screwed into my head. (Right) Sitting in a chair at home, in the cage—the Halo. Still weak in arms and hands.

IN A HALO BUT HE'S NO ANGEL

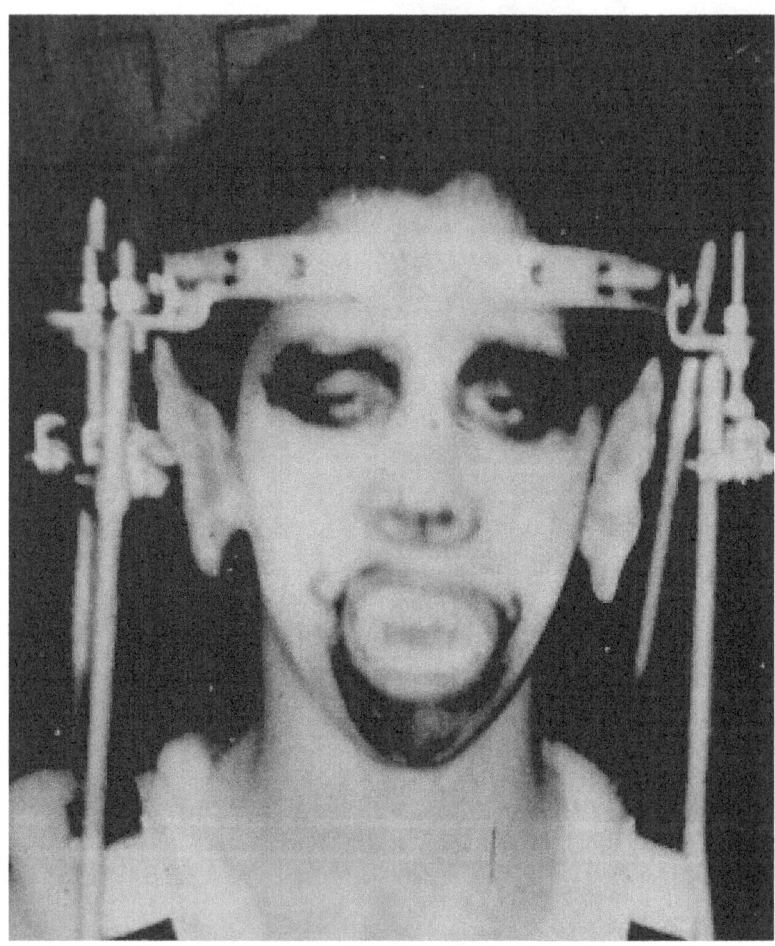

Halloween...My very strange sense of humor was to look like this. I thought it was hilarious. It stormed that night and I walked around trick or treating in a metal cage, like a lightning rod. People thought the Halo was part of my costume.

Young Love...I fell in love with Stacy (top) while she was still in high school and I was in college. She was great girl. A smart girl. After a year, Stacy found someone else.

Leah (bottom), a beautiful Greek girl was my next love. We were together for a year and a half, here at Benchwarmer's Bar in Lawrence watching Jayhawk basketball. Leah planned her future, but I was adrift. She broke it off with me.

Me. On Skis!...A ski pass came with my job in Vail, Colorado. With all four limbs affected by my spinal cord injury, I learned to ski. I had the time of my life, alone and ski-ing down a snow covered mountain while screaming, Oh, this is fun!

Family of 3...Mom, Hank (me in the middle). Having fun on a night out at a local restaurant.

Q&A...Listening to an athlete form a question in one of many presentations for the Kansas University Athletics Department. Students learn from me and I learn from them.

Molly...Molly (left) looking dressed up and grown up before singing in a school concert. She performs and sings at school and in public, like student singers did in the TV show, Glee.

Molly in her sixth-grade class photo.

Faces...Molly and I are both smiling, but we gave the pumpkin a mean-looking face that year. Carving a big pumpkin is one of our favorite things to do together for Halloween.

Made in the USA
Coppell, TX
10 October 2025

61104108R10100